Listeni

Listening to your Life

*30 ways to discern direction
for your future*

Julia Mourant

CANTERBURY
PRESS
Norwich

© Julia Mourant 2016

First published in 2016 by the Canterbury Press Norwich
Editorial office
3rd Floor, Invicta House
108–114 Golden Lane
London EC1Y 0TG, UK

Canterbury Press is an imprint of Hymns Ancient & Modern Ltd
(a registered charity)
13A Hellesdon Park Road, Norwich,
Norfolk NR6 5DR, UK

www.canterburypress.co.uk

British Library Cataloguing in Publication data

A catalogue record for this book is available
from the British Library

978 1-84825-878-5

Typeset by Regent Typesetting
Printed and bound in Great Britain by
CPI Group (UK) Ltd

Contents

Introduction

'What on earth am I here for?' This question appears in our dreams, and presents itself at critical junctions and transitions in our lives. Births, marriages and deaths; moves, losses and illness; great achievements and shattering failures – all bring us back to this central question.

Some of us find the courage to make life-changing decisions about what we believe really matters, choices that friends, colleagues and family may admire and be inspired by. Whenever someone does something surprising or daring, there are always people who find the courage to begin making their own changes. They may think, 'I could do that!' or it may dawn on them that they are in need of some change too. Others, however, will find the possibility of change too challenging and uncomfortable, and so bury it for another day, a day that may never come. Radical change comes at a price, and although some people will encourage you and say, 'Good for you!', perhaps you feel that others will misunderstand or even judge you. Sadly, some of these people might even be a bit jealous, though they may not be fully aware of it. Frustrated, perhaps even feeling trapped, they find it hard to believe that there are real choices to be made; they continue on their own path or treadmill while resenting those who appear to have more freedom.

Appearances can be deceptive. Circumstances may not make it easy, but there are always inner choices to be made about 'how' to live, even if the 'where' and 'when' are determined for us. It is certainly true that some aspects of our lives simply cannot be altered. Nevertheless, when we take a close look from a different perspective, we may begin to see that we could change more than we realize. People of faith put these questions in a framework of belief, know their identity in God, and find hope and meaning in being part of a bigger picture. Yet for each individual, the question of who I am and what my life means remains. It is quite possible to be deeply rooted in your faith, be a person of prayer, belong to a worshipping community, faithfully serve and give of yourself and yet, and yet ... still be wondering: 'What on earth am I here for?' You may already sense that life is not 'all about me', and feel sure there is *something* you should be doing, if only you could discover what it is.

Whether you are already exploring new possibilities or just waking up to the idea that there is something more for you to discover, this book will help you answer that multilayered question of meaning, purpose and direction, which could just as easily be called 'vocation'. Vocation is what calls you, draws you, compels and inspires you as the reason to get out of bed in the morning and keep breathing.

Vocation is not about 'what I want to be when I grow up' or finding a better job, but a rich tapestry that draws together experience, gifts, relationships, learning and context. It is not about fulfilment in just one aspect of life, but about the fullness of becoming all that is already God-given within us. It is possible to live vocationally, with a sense of meaning, purpose and direction, even in circumstances where there is little choice or control over the details of our lives. Sometimes what we need is not external change but an inner change of perspective. Conversely, a change of inner perspective can liberate and motivate us for change in ways we never imagined possible.

The reflective exercises in this book offer fresh perspectives from which to consider these questions. They offer creative and interactive ways of reflecting on your life, experience and vocation, enabling you to consider many aspects of your life and to pay attention, to listen to your life, where the Spirit is always at work.

At times there is focus on the past or the future, but we always come back to the present. It is only in the present that, by the grace of God, we discern and we act.

The spiritual writer Thich Nhat Hanh reminds us that: 'Our appointment with life is in the present moment. The place of our appointment is right here, in this very place.'[1] This does not mean that the past and future are of no account or do not matter, but we can only actually live in the present, which holds all the past and future. He continues:

> The best way of preparing for the future is to take good care of the present, because we know that if the present is made up of the past, then the future will be made up of the present. All we need to be responsible for is the present moment. Only the present is within our reach. To care for the present is to care for the future.

Use these reflections to listen to your life with hope. You are invited to celebrate the past, and where necessary to recycle it. Imagine the future creatively and expansively rather than fearfully. To be fully alive is to be present, listening, and able to live each moment with a sense of vocation. 'We do not have to die to enter the Kingdom of Heaven. In fact we have to be fully alive.'[2]

1 Thich Nhat Hanh, *Essential Writings*, Orbis Books, 2001, p. 41.
2 Thich Nhat Hanh, *Essential Writings*, p. 23.

How to use this book

This book is for everyone considering the meaning, purpose and direction of life; in other words, if you are seeking to live vocationally, in harmony with the deepest sense of call in your life. It is written from within the Christian tradition but the reflections here could be used in any framework of belief or spirituality. The reflections could be part of a regular devotional pattern, or you could take the book on a retreat or quiet day. They are suitable for anyone just beginning to explore a spiritual path, as well as for those who have been doing so for many years. These reflections invite you into a sacred space in which you can encounter God, in the midst of your life, your experience, your prayer. The themes here can never be either too simple or too complicated, because you bring the raw material and you choose the depth and direction of your prayerful reflection. This book is for anyone who is ready to respond to an invitation to listen to God – by listening to life. God is to be encountered in the detail, the frustration, the joys and sorrows, successes and apparent dead ends in our lives. Listening to life means listening to our experience, including nature, poetry, art, Scripture, travel, relationships, work, and whatever else comes our way.

This book is designed for individuals to use, not as a course, but as a resource for prayerful reflection, whether regularly or occasionally. The material can also be adapted for use in groups, with some careful preparation and explanation. There is more about this in the following introductory material, and in the notes for each reflection.

Listening to your life

The edges of our lives – fully experienced, suffered and enjoyed – lead us back to the centre and the essence.[3]

Where is life going, and what does it mean? How do we think about vocation? How can we know what God may be calling us to do in our lives? How do we know if any choice, decision or option is really the way to go or just a momentary fantasy? Peering into the future, we wonder about what paths to follow. At the same time, looking back, we have much to be thankful for, yet still wonder if we missed a turning somewhere. All this distracts from the present moment, of course, which is the only moment in which we can actually live out a sense of purpose, meaning or vocation. We can think, overthink, and think ourselves round in circles, pondering options and possibilities, getting caught up in practicalities and obstacles and impediments. We are full of enthusiasm one day, but the next morning not sure if this is all in our mind and not of the Spirit. How can we know the difference between an authentic call and our own desires? Can we trust the joy and hope within us? We can end up weary, confused and no further forward, trying to 'listen' but hearing only our own anxieties and questions. We may believe that God is speaking to us but we are not sure what it means, or whether we have heard right. Perhaps the call is for someone else, or for some future time. Can we make anything at all of our lives?

At such times the best way forward may be to stop 'thinking' at all and approach the questions from a different angle. Thinking is important, but there is also a deep inner wisdom within us, given

---

3 Richard Rohr, *Everything Belongs*, Crossroad, 1999, p. 17.

by God, in a place where we know more than we know, without knowing how we know. This place of intuition, wisdom, the voice of the Spirit, where life experience is integrated, is somewhere most of us probably don't visit enough. The language in this deep place often speaks of hopes, dreams and metaphors; of desires, memory, colour and imagination, rather than of logic and lists. It is a place for stillness and silence and slowing down. Through our imagination, God may surprise, challenge and transform us in ways we could not possibly have foreseen.

This space could perhaps be described as 'contemplative', although this is a word that can be used in a number of ways. We hear it used to describe anything from a particular tradition of prayer to a reflective act of worship, or an introverted personality. The reflections in this book are 'contemplative' in the sense that they encourage the reader to enter a different kind of space, beyond the thoughts and words that we may begin with, as the only starting place we have. The reflections and exercises in this book offer some initial ideas, perhaps words or pictures, but these only represent a doorway leading into a space where you will put this on one side and encounter the Spirit in your deepest place.

The writer and mystic Thomas Merton looked at the nature of 'contemplation' from many angles. For him it meant a particular path of prayer, but one that was deeply connected with the world, life and vocation.

> Contemplation is also the response to a call; a call from him who has no voice, and yet speaks in everything that is, and who, most of all, speaks in the depths of our own being; for we ourselves are words of his. But we are words that are meant to respond to him, to answer to him, to echo him, and even in some ways to contain him and signify him.[4]

The God-language is that of Merton's time and his world, but there is a truth here: that however we understand or speak of

---

4 Thomas Merton, *New Seeds of Contemplation*, Burns and Oates, 1999 (first published 1962), p. 14.

God, a response to God is fundamental to the meaning of life. We are called to listen, hear, reflect and echo; to live as a sign and invitation for others into God-encounter. This is the meaning of vocation. The spiritual writer Richard Rohr puts it like this:

> Prayer is not primarily saying words or thinking thoughts. It is, rather, a stance. It's a way of living in the Presence, even enjoying the Presence. The full contemplative is not just aware of the Presence, but trusts, allows, and delights in it.[5]

The material in this book invites you to engage with that Presence and prayerfully respond in the present moment, to offer up the past for all that it is, and to trust in and hope for the future, knowing that your life has meaning, purpose and direction in which you can live and breathe. You will be living vocationally.

---

5 Rohr, *Everything Belongs*, p. 29.

Using the reflections

Most of us live such busy lives that we rarely take time to reflect on the riches buried in our hearts and in our traditions – riches that help us discover who we really are, and to find meaning and purpose within our seemingly random, fragmented and ordinary existence; riches that help us make those soulful reconnections that so many of us, deep down, yearn to make – with the world around us, with each other, with ourselves, and with the higher power often called God.[6]

The reflections in this book make use of simple ideas and metaphors, often ordinary and everyday; some are quite familiar and may well have been used elsewhere. It is natural to draw on the earth's times, seasons and horizons as ways of looking at life. A metaphor is a powerful tool for shedding new light on certain aspects of our experiences, our questions and relationships, because it offers a different perspective, another angle. A metaphor acts as a kind of mirror; it reflects something of the object we are considering. But it is not a perfect mirror so we must play with it a little. A metaphor is never an exact match, merely another way of looking – a window. These reflections are not ends in themselves; they do not constitute a programme or course and they do not follow any particular order. They are recyclable, in the sense of being suitable as a starting point for prayer again and again; on each occasion some completely fresh insight or challenge or reassurance may emerge. Every time you consider the question, 'What time is it in your life?' for example, you are likely to have a completely different response. On another day, the wind will blow from another direction, you will be living with different questions

---

6 Brian Draper, *Spiritual Intelligence*, Lion, 2009, p. 12.

and priorities, and the insights you have will be just as 'true', but also just as partial. Metaphors allow us to live with contradiction and paradox. I may reflect one day that my life feels like 10 a.m., the next it may seem more like 4 p.m. Both may be 'true' and each may evoke a particular sense of vocation, but nevertheless I may be able to weave both perspectives into my daily life.

The series of reflections in this book are written primarily for individuals to use, but could be adapted for a group as part of a quiet day or retreat. Some might be suitable for a reflective pause on a day for those exploring vocation, or as part of a day for spiritual directors. They require very little in the way of materials, many requiring only a large sheet of paper and some coloured pens. You sometimes need a pair of scissors, ruler and pencil, and occasionally one or two other everyday items are useful. A candle may help you enter a meditative space for listening to your own depths and the whisper of the Spirit, or to create a still place in which to pray through what has challenged or surprised you, evoking thanksgiving, intercession or a specific response to God.

In themselves the exercises are extremely simple; there is nothing clever, remarkable or even 'deeply spiritual' about them. The real work of these reflections is not in the ideas, the writing or drawing, or what appears on the paper at all, but rather in the barely discernible spaces so easily missed when one is bent on finishing a task or doing it right. One might be tempted to 'do' one of these reflections in 10 minutes, but you would quite possibly be none the wiser after that time. It is undoubtedly true that sometimes by the grace of God we have a flash of insight when we are at our least prayerful or receptive, but on the whole, time and space deepen our receptivity and capacity for transformation. The really creative opportunity is the emptiness of the contemplative space where there can be permission to slow down and find the courage to ponder with a blank sheet. In that place, we can engage with all our ifs, buts, and maybes; our memories, daydreams and fears. We give voice to what is within us and offer it to God honestly, openly and expectantly. The purpose of these reflections is not to 'do' or 'think' anything; by a process of focused and reflective doing and thinking we can perhaps move into another room, where we know what we know without knowing how we know it, and we hear what we hear without knowing how we hear it, and we are utterly transformed.

These exercises are not an end in themselves, but an invitation into a still, listening place, where you are receptive to the stirrings of the soul that are so easily dismissed or discounted when life is speeding along. The 'work' is done in the spaces when little, even nothing, seems to be happening, when you are pondering what to write, or realizing that what you have written is a complete surprise. The reflections offer a skeleton frame, some scaffolding; it is not the doing of the task that is transformative but the encounter with the Spirit that takes place when you use the task as a threshold to a place of encounter.

There is, of course, always the danger of being overly self-absorbed, so it's a good idea to surround these reflections with prayer for wisdom to listen to the invitation of the Spirit, who whispers renewal and healing. Above all, there should be a note of joy and light about inner work like this, even when challenging or uncomfortable moments present themselves, perhaps tears. Tears can be cleansing and bring relief, and are not to be feared in prayerful reflection. However, if you find the reflections becoming heavy or oppressive, stop what you are doing right away, put the book away and take some time to be still in a sense of God's life-giving presence. Go outside and feel the warmth of the sun on your skin, or do something creative that gives you joy. Know when you need to talk with someone else. A time of deep reflection at the right time will be a gift, but the Spirit blows where the Spirit wills, and God does not always speak at the time of our choosing, so approach these reflections with a light touch.

You can use the reflections in any order. Some will appeal or resonate more than others at particular times, so go with whatever draws you as you listen for the nudging of the Spirit. Those that do not seem at all relevant or useful one day may turn out to offer just the right prompt on another occasion. However, once you have begun a reflection try not to be tempted to give up on it if it does not seem immediately fruitful. There is more happening in the spaces and silences than you can know.

Preparing a space

Moments of awakening come to us as a gift. Frequently, they arise when we manage to stop talking or even thinking and start listening instead. And very often they come to us quietly, almost insignificantly. These are the times to really listen up.[7]

You need very little in order to engage with these reflections, but there are a few essential things:

What you need

- Time
- A few simple materials
- A quiet, safe space
- A journal or notebook

In addition, you may find it helpful to have someone to talk with, such as a spiritual director. This should be someone you trust, who will listen to whatever you want to share, without jumping in with advice or interpretation. You can find more information about finding a spiritual director in the Resources section at the end of this book.

Time

The amount of time could be anything from half an hour or so (depending on the exercise), to a whole day. It is important not to be in a rush, and to be able to set aside the time without other

7 Draper, *Spiritual Intelligence*, p. 24.

distractions. Be somewhere you are not likely to be disturbed, away from the immediate intrusion of other people, phones and emails. Know that for this next little while you can relax into being in God's presence without interruption. You need enough time not only to do the suggested reflection, but to become still and centred before you begin, and to reflect afterwards on what you want to take forward. You may want to record the experience in your journal, write a prayer, or just sit for a while with what you have felt or 'heard' and let it soak into you.

Some simple materials

Make sure that you have what you need before you begin. Most of the exercises need just paper and pens, perhaps pencil, scissors and ruler. Some people like to use a candle during their reflection or afterwards, so have one ready and something to light it with. Remember to extinguish it later, although it's a good idea anyway to place it on something that won't catch fire. Occasionally exercises suggest other everyday items; one reflection suggests going online; but this is made clear in the introduction to each reflection.

The paper required should be large – most of these exercises work best on at least A2 size, so you have plenty of room to work with and you are not squashing your ideas into corners or running out of space. This feeling of having lots of space is really important. If you are tempted to use a small piece of paper, you may fill it up in a few minutes. Then your mind will tell you that you are 'done', and the listening, open space within you will subconsciously shut down. The white space on the page is an invitation and a prayer, a sign of your willingness to receive what is new, surprising and challenging. Another reason for using big paper is that you can write or draw on different scales, from very large to very small. You will have plenty of room to add symbols, pictures, smiley faces, question marks or anything else that occurs to you. This means that your heart, mind and body are engaged in a completely different way from scribbling on the back of an envelope (though that can be useful sometimes too). Be bold, put some energy and life into what you are expressing, and if that seems difficult, consider why. Let your inner wisdom prompt you to write in huge letters if it feels 'big', or needs to become 'big'. Give yourself permission to write something tiny in the corner if this is honest or challenging. You can take all this into prayer later, when you put down the pens and see what has emerged.

Most of the exercises suggest using coloured pens. You could, of course, do them with a single colour if that is all that is available, but this could be rather one-dimensional. Colour allows for expression and contrast, and your choice of colour may be quite important to you. One thing to bear in mind, though, is that the purpose of these exercises is not to produce a beautiful work of art. You may take pleasure in creating an end result that is quite artistic, or you might pay no attention to the 'look' of your work at all. You do not need to be remotely artistic to engage fully with these reflections; in fact, an attempt to produce a beautiful picture may be an unhelpful distraction. Being able to draw may actively get in the way. One participant at a workshop spent a whole afternoon creating a beautiful drawing with considerable attention to detail, but found the limited range of simple colours on the table frustrating and limiting. Would a greater range of subtle hues have led to deeper spiritual work? Possibly, but the artistic desire for a lovely picture could just as easily be a distraction from the real work. That said, get yourself a decent pack of felt pens with a good choice of colours. Don't just rummage in the toy box or the back of the kitchen drawer for something that will just about do. You will enjoy the work more if you are not scrubbing away at the paper searching for signs of life from your marker. But in the end, the subtlety of colour and the technical merit of the drawing are not important. It does not matter if your writing makes no sense to anyone else and your attempt to draw a bird or a house is laughable. Your paper won't be seen by anyone else, unless you choose to share it with someone you trust, such as a spiritual director. It is not what is on the paper that matters, it is in the spaces around your thinking, praying, writing, noticing, that an encounter with the Spirit takes place.

Plan to actually 'do' these reflections, not just think about them and make a few halfhearted scribbles. Reading the book without engaging with the 'work' is like reading a recipe book, very interesting but not at all nourishing until you do the cooking, which may not turn out anything like the book. No one is watching, and if you have never done this sort of thing before, prepare to be surprised at what emerges. There is something sacramental, intentional and powerful about committing your heart and soul to colour and paper. There are things that may be hard to name, difficult to write, or that do not reveal their secrets until we put them on the page, perhaps with colour and metaphor. One has to move beyond ideas to the choice of words, their colour, size and shape, pictures, names. The physical activity of using scissors, for example, slows you down and gives your hands something to do. This can be important for those who do not find it easy to pray by simply sitting very still in a chair. Approach the physicality of drawing, cutting, making lines, writing, slowly and with care. It is a way of praying in which you are saying, 'I am here, I am paying attention to this space and to the call of the Spirit right here, right now, with this paper, and these colours, and my life as it is, not how I would like it to be.'

A quiet, safe space

The most important thing you will need is yourself, and the capacity to enter into a reflective and prayerful space, so consider what you, as an individual, require in order to enter such a space. You may have somewhere suitable at home, or you may like to go out somewhere not too far away, but removed from possible interruptions or distractions. You could plan a quiet day or retreat, perhaps at a retreat house – or anywhere where you know you can settle into a sense of God's presence. For some, even a coffee shop is a 'retreat' space, which can engage you in a different kind of solitude or presence. You might struggle to spread out a large sheet of paper, but it could be a starting point for reflection.

Decide how long you have to spend on the exercise. If you are away for a whole day, or on a longer retreat, will you include other activities during this time, such as prayer, walking, or creative activity? If you have time for these, they may help you to prepare for and then integrate the work around a particular reflection.

As you approach your chosen reflection, try to enter into an inner place of spiritual awareness, in whatever way you may be familiar with. This might mean lighting a candle or some incense, using a prayer book, reading some Scripture, listening to music, or just slowing down and noticing your breathing, your surroundings, and entering more fully into the present moment. You do not have to 'come' into God's presence, only remember that you are already there. Faith and spirituality writer Ronald Rolheiser expresses it like this:

> The struggle to experience God is not so much one of God's presence or absence as it is one of the presence or absence of God *in our awareness*. God is always present, but we are not always present to God ... God can be very present in an event but we can be so preoccupied and focussed on our headaches, heartaches, tasks, daydreams and distracting restlessness that we can be oblivious to that presence.[8]

The Resources section at the end of this book offers a few ideas if you want to explore meditation practices as ways of becoming still and centred. You will notice that the 'instructions' for each reflection include encouragement to take time to become still. Don't even think about writing or drawing anything until you know you have crossed, in your own way, a threshold into a greater stillness and receptivity. You may still be aware of outside distractions, but you are slowing down and allowing space for the Spirit to have a voice. As you approach this space, come pre-

---

8 Ronald Rolheiser, *The Shattered Lantern*, Crossroad, 2004, p. 22.

pared to be present for as long as you need to, and especially to be present in the spaces where nothing much seems to be happening.

A journal or notebook

You may find it helpful to write about your journey through these pages in a journal or notebook, noting down your thoughts, prayers and inner responses. You might use a beautiful notebook or quite an ordinary one; it might have lined pages, or blank ones, good for doodles or pasting things in. You could create an electronic journal. You might write in the journal every day, or just occasionally. There is no right approach. Even if you do not use a journal regularly, you may find some benefit in jotting down your thoughts and prayers as you engage with the exercises in this book. A journal or private notebook is very personal and sacred, so make sure you keep it in a safe place where others are not going to find it and become curious about it. The most liberating thing about a journal is that, if you are willing, you can use it to tell the truth. You can be honest and put into words the things that are hard to name; you can see the words on the page and hear them in your heart. This is your reality; your journey with God can only start here.

> The authentic spiritual life finds its basis in the human condition. The spiritual life is not lived outside, before, after, or beyond our everyday existence. No, the spiritual life can be real only as it is lived in the midst of the pains and joys of the here and now. Therefore, we need to begin with a careful look at the way we think, speak, feel, and act from hour to hour, day to day, week to week, and year to year, in order to become more fully aware of our hunger for the Spirit. As long as we have only a vague inner feeling of discontent with our present way of living, and only an indefinite desire for 'things spiritual', our lives will continue to stagnate in generalised melancholy. We often say, 'I am not very happy. I am not content with the way my life is going.

I am not really joyful or peaceful. But I don't know how things could be different, and I guess I have to be realistic and accept my life as it is.' It is this mood of resignation that prevents us from actively naming our reality, articulating our experience, and moving more deeply into the life of the Spirit.[9]

Spiritual accompaniment

The very first place you will take your reflections to will be the place of prayer in your heart, pondering the mysteries that will continue to be at work within long after you have finished your time of reflection and returned to ordinary demands. A deepening sense of the work of the Spirit, a focusing on the sense of vocation: these are tender plants that need time. A woman early in pregnancy will speak to no one about the new life she carries, because once she shares her wondrous secret those around her will begin to offer not only the support she will welcome in due course, but also stories and opinions that may be intrusive and advice that she is not ready to receive. There is a moment for God to speak in the dark, and in those starlight hours we wait in joyful and silent hope, offering not even our 'yes' but perhaps only 'here I am'.

However, there may come a point at which you may find it helpful to have someone to talk with, such as a spiritual director. This should be someone you trust, who will listen to whatever you want to share, without jumping in with advice or interpretation. A spiritual director will listen while you consider the question, 'How am I responding to God in my life right now?' She or he won't tell you what to do, give you the answers, or judge you, but will help to create a sacred and spacious place in which to listen to God, to yourself and to your life. A spiritual director takes you seriously, but also helps you to laugh at yourself. You can find information about finding a spiritual director in the Resources section at the end of this book.

9 Henri Nouwen, *Spiritual Formation*, SPCK, 2011, p. xxii.

For most of us the beginning point is at the edges. This reality, felt and not denied, suffering and enjoyed, becomes the royal road to the centre. In other words, reality itself, our reality, my limited and sometimes misinterpreted experience, still becomes the revelatory place for God.[10]

10 Rohr, *Everything Belongs*, p. 17.

Using the reflections with a group

Practicalities

Most of the reflections in this book can be adapted for use with a group, and there are relevant notes on this at the end of each one. The materials are simple and easy to prepare, but think through the practicalities of what you need, the space you will be using, and exactly what you need to have prepared beforehand. While a few of the exercises could be done on A4 paper, most work best with at least A2 size, so you need to think about whether people will need tables to work on. Be careful about working on the floor; this may suit some people but not everyone, and felt pens can bleed through paper onto carpet and may be impossible to clean off. The work is personal and people may not wish to be overlooked by others, so it is best to have plenty of breakout space. On a retreat, people can use their own rooms, which is helpful from a practical point of view. Gather plenty of pens and scissors, or ask people to bring them on the day.

Introducing the reflection

Introduce the exercise by offering an opportunity to slow down and 'arrive' in the space. If you are used to leading groups then you will have your own way of doing this. You could use a stillness meditation, a short liturgy, some Bible reading, poetry, music, prayer or, of course, silence. As you explain the exercise, aim to be simple, clear, and inspire confidence, especially in the following ways:

- There is no right way; this is not a task to please the 'teacher'.
- If you interpret the reflection in your own way, that is fine.
- You do not have to share anything unless you choose to do so.
- If you feel that the reflection is genuinely not helpful, or some element of it is distressing or disturbing you, take responsibility for yourself, and stop, do something else or speak to someone.

When you have explained the exercise, allow a brief time for quick questions and try to respond in a manner that is reassuring and deals kindly with any insecurity or anxiety. Be clear about how much time the group have, where you want them to go and what you want them to do at the end of that time. It is usually a good idea to plan to draw the group back together, even if not for long, so that people can 'land' any immediate responses and you can be sure that no one has found the reflection destabilizing in an unhelpful way.

Reflecting afterwards

When you bring the group back together, there are a number of approaches you can use. Depending on the size of the group, you might want to ask openly for any comments or responses. Encourage contributions offering a sense of the experience of engaging with the reflection, rather than detailed explanations of what people have put down on paper. It is important to dispel any uneasy expectation that everyone has to 'show and tell'. Invite sharing around questions such as, 'What was it like to do that?' rather than 'What did you do?' One way to avoid lengthy individual reporting is to ask for one-word responses. Give permission, if you need to, for difficult feelings such as 'perturbed' as well as responses such as 'amazing'.

You will probably have already mentioned confidentiality but if you need to remind the group of this do so, pointing out that respecting each other's space means leaving in the room what has been shared in that session, and not initiating a conversation at coffee time in response to something shared earlier. If appropriate, divide the group into pairs, threes or small groups. If you do this, be clear about what the task is. You might be asking them to share what the experience was like for them, not necessarily 'what' went on the paper. This can be deeper than simply showing each other their papers, a conversation which may consist of narrative without reflection. Be clear about the ground rules, which might include:

- listening without comment;
- noticing but not interpreting;
- using only 'I' language rather than 'you' talk;
- avoiding assumptions or judgements;
- holding back from giving advice or sharing own experience in response to others.

These are all simple common-sense pointers and principles, and group leaders will have their own ways of working. The important thing is to ensure that the space is safe for everyone at every level, while not, of course, creating such a comfortable zone that God cannot get in to challenge, surprise, call, or reassure.

I

Compass

The points of the compass – north, south, east and west – have long been a natural focus for thinking about life, meaning and purpose. The seasons, too, raise the same kinds of questions within us as we consider winter, spring, summer and autumn and what these times say to us and require of us.

This reflection uses the idea of four directions that we may gaze towards: four different horizons. It can be fruitful to pay attention to each one of these at a time and let the questions, which may be deeply uncomfortable, present themselves. Each horizon has the potential to offer a particular kind of invitation. These invitations do not always offer themselves up immediately, horizons are to be gazed at, wondered at. We need to allow our gaze to be attuned to a different perspective, to subtle changes in the light, that we might find courage and grace for the welcoming, the celebrating and the surrendering.

What you need

- A large sheet of paper, preferably at least A2
- Coloured pens
- A candle and some matches

The exercise

Fold your paper into four sections then open it out again. Mark the sections as north, south, east and west. Be still and consider prayerfully each of the following horizons and the questions that each direction presents. Take plenty of time with each section, and when you have finished one, do not be in a hurry to rush on to the next but allow further thoughts, perhaps surprising ones, to arise. Allow each horizon to 'speak' to you; note the inner feelings, emotions and physical responses that are evoked within you. You can do them in any order, but the order suggested below has a natural progression.

Do not try to answer all of the following questions; they are only suggestions. Allow yourself to be drawn to any questions that the Spirit is stirring up within you. These may not be the easiest ones to consider so do not be too quick to dismiss anything. Be open to reassurance, celebration and challenge.

North

- What is stable in my life?
- What gives me a sense of direction?
- What can I truly rely on?
- What gives me a sense of rootedness?
- Are there certain 'givens' in my life, which I cannot change or escape from?

South

- What is truly flourishing for me right now?
- Where am I seeing fruitfulness, harvest, joy?
- Are earlier hopes, dreams and promises being lived out?
- What deeply touches my soul with hope?

West

- What things in my life are coming to an end?
- What am I glad to give up, move beyond, get past?
- What is being taken from me?
- What must I lay down with thanksgiving?
- What memories am I treasuring?

East

- What new things might be over the horizon?
- Where am I waiting in the dark for a new dawn?
- What barely discernible glimpses of change or promise can I see?
- What do I hope for?
- Where am I now called to invest my time, my energy, my love?

It is not possible to look in all four directions at once. Where is my attention mostly focused at this time in my life? Do I need to take more account of other horizons?

Reflection

This exercise may evoke bittersweet emotions of wistfulness, longing, loss, nostalgia and memory. But it will also call forth new hope and courage for the future, if you can turn your gaze with thanksgiving towards the eastern horizon where the sun rises without fail for us as long as we live and breathe. Even then, the horizon we watched will be watched by others we have loved and given life to.

Spread out your paper somewhere flat. Take a candle and place it in the centre, where the folds meet. Open your hands in prayer and offer each of these horizons to God, finishing with a prayer that you may gaze into the east with new hope, ready for a new sense of call.

Consider these words:

There is a time in life when you expect the world to be always full of new things. And then comes a day when you realise that is not how it will be at all. You see that life will become a thing made of holes. Absences. Losses. Things that were there and are no longer. And you realise, too, that you have to grow around and between the gaps, though you can put your hand out to where things were and feel that tense, shining dullness of the space where the memories are.[11]

Can I grow around and between the gaps? Do I have the courage to face fully into the east and welcome new things?

There are ways to celebrate endings and beginnings liturgically, if this is useful. Prayer resources such as Dorothy McRae-McMahon's *Prayers for Life's Particular Moments* or *Human Rites* by Hannah Ward and Jennifer Wild offer lots of ideas.

You can find a version of this reflection in *The Discerning Heart* by Wilkie and Noreen Cannon Au, as well as further pointers and exercises for reflection on listening to the Spirit.

In a group

This can be a powerful exercise that really needs plenty of time. You can give the group one section at a time and then bring them back for sharing and listening, if this is appropriate. Follow the rhythm of north, south, west and east because this allows people to start with a sense of rootedness (north) before moving into celebration (south). Any sense of loss (west) is then held between that celebration and the new hope of the dawn (east). Finish with a prayerful time of reflection that allows everyone to let go of the emotions and thoughts that have arisen for them.

---

11 Helen Macdonald, *H is for Hawk*, Jonathan Cape, 2014, p. 171.

2

Compost

Compost is a miraculous thing. You can make it by collecting organic waste such as vegetable peelings and tea bags, banana skins, straw from the rabbit hutch and even fluff from the tumble drier. You can add weeds (but be careful – not if they have seeds); and a good layer of grass cuttings will help to heat it all up nicely. Compost is pretty independent but it benefits from a little over-sight; a random pile of organic material won't compost as quickly as a properly contained mix with the right proportions of green and brown, hard and soft. Compost needs some moisture and warmth, and certainly needs time. But given favourable con-ditions, worms (and maybe beetles or even grass snakes) and a little love, in due course you will have a fragrant crumbly result that will enhance your garden as mulch, soil enricher or growing medium. What's not to like? Better still, unless the garden centre persuaded you to buy special compost-making preparations to speed things along, it's free.

Compost can be said to be a lot like life, and it's not difficult to see why. 'Life compost', as it might be called, is as essential to vo-cation as organic matter is to growing things in the garden or field.

One very common question that crops up as people start to explore a sense of vocation is this: 'Am I capable and equipped?'

And a related question is: 'Will my previous mistakes, wrong turnings, difficult experiences or various incapacities get in the way?'

Vocation, of whatever sort, whether to a ministry, or to a work role (voluntary or paid), or to turning up to a particular place, time or relationship, needs roots. Anything that is done from a sense of call needs to be sustained by some form of nourishment, which gives growth and strength. It is amazing how rich compost is made from the most extraordinary waste, recycled into an unrecognizable form. The wonderful thing is that when you look at a wheelbarrow full of beautiful compost, it is still essentially made up of the same materials that went in to start with. The banana skins and tea bags are still 'there', you just can't see them any more because they have been utterly transformed.

Life can feel as though it contains a lot of unrecycled waste. It gets in the way, keeps us awake, makes us feel guilty or inadequate, and however well things are going, and whatever encouraging things are said to you, there may be the tendency to think 'if you only knew'. It's common for people to go through life feeling like a fraud, convinced they will be found out and shamed any day, it's only a matter of time. However, we can get this all upside down and inside out. The organic waste is not what gets in the way; this is what makes vocation possible. The important part is the offering up of what looks like rubbish and waste, subjecting it to a natural process so that moisture, warmth and a bit of time get to work on it. The life equivalent of these things could include compassion towards self and others, or a willingness to smile at previous foolishness. Some things might seem truly terrible and you wonder how they can ever be composted. Whether these are events that happened, or things for which you feel personally responsible, all you can do is keep asking God to recycle them. If you wake in the night, full of anguish and regret, there is only one prayer to pray, and it is a very good one: 'Recycle this, God. Take it, compost it, do something with it, because I certainly cannot.'

Whatever needs to be composted may not disappear, but it will be transformed. Here is an exercise to help you chuck your waste into the compost bin.

What you need

- A large sheet of paper, at least A2
- Coloured pens

The exercise

On your paper, draw the outline of a traditional square compost bin made of wooden planks. If that sounds too artistic just draw a big square with a few lines on the front to represent the planks. Now, in the compost bin, with pens, colours, words or pictures, just as you like, write all the things that you feel need composting, what feels rubbishy, seems like a waste, is surrounded with regret, negativity, blame, shame and heartache. Big or small, from a disastrous life choice to the comment you wish you had not made, in they go. Everything that you feel might get in the way of finding or following any sense of vocation, or perhaps even being useful to God at all, can go in.

When you cannot think of anything else, put a lid on top of the compost bin. Draw a lid, or just a thick black line. An old carpet on top is one way gardeners keep the heat in and the rain out. You are done; all this is now with God for composting. Fold your paper up so that the picture is on the inside, and write 'Recycling' on the outside. You might like to put this paper away somewhere, or tuck it in your journal or Bible. You could burn it if you wish, and put the ash in the garden or in a pot of bulbs. Or you can recycle it in the following way. In the autumn, take a large flower pot and put some compost in the bottom. Now shred your paper, or rip it up very small, and lay the pieces on top of this layer of compost. Mix it in a bit, then add another layer of compost. Plant some bulbs such as daffodils or tulips, or corms such as snowdrops or crocus. Another layer of compost on these will keep them snug, then put the pot somewhere sheltered to catch the spring sunshine. The bulb roots will grow down into the compost; then, when spring has faded and the flowers are gone, find a place in your garden to replant the whole lot to flower for years to come.

Prayer

God, sometimes I really wonder what to do with all this stuff. How can I be useful when I have got things wrong, made humiliating mistakes? How can I be fit for ministry with my circumstances and difficulties and history? But because of these things, perhaps I understand life and people and even myself in a different way. I can notice things I would not have seen. I have made mistakes I won't make again (though I am sure to make others). Maybe I will be able to encourage others who have had similar disasters. Let me be a walking invitation not to give up or do yourself down, living evidence that God recycles everything.

Further reflection

I believe contemplation shows us that nothing inside us is as bad as our hatred and denial of it. Hating and denying only complicates our problems. All of it is grist for the mill. Everything belongs. God uses everything. There are no dead ends. There is no wasted energy. Everything is recycled.[12]

You must travel throughout all of time and space to know the true impact of any event. Every success contains some difficulties, and every failure contributes to increased wisdom or future success. Every event is both fortunate and unfortunate, good and bad exist only in our perceptions.[13]

It can be hard to stop 'beating ourselves up', but it might help to think about something that once seemed disastrous. What is my perspective on it now? How have I seen the natural process of composting at work in my life?

---

12 Rohr, *Everything Belongs*, p. 111.
13 Thich Nhat Hanh, *Essential Writings*, p. 49.

In a group

Introduce the exercise as described here and allow people plenty of time to go and work alone. Be aware that some things are very deep and difficult and the idea of 'composting' these may seem too superficial. While there is a theological truth about redemption and resurrection at work here, serious situations such as abuse, bereavement, addiction and criminality cannot lightly or easily be 'recycled' and it would be insensitive to suggest that this metaphor can be applied in a 'sticking plaster' fashion. The reflection is not intended to offer deep therapy, merely to suggest an alternative perspective. If the metaphor is not appropriate, it should not be forced but abandoned. The best approach is to listen and acknowledge that this is not the right time and place for the language of recycling. There will be other ways to address certain issues and experiences and the individuals need to discern and choose what these may be.

3

Paths, roads and tracks

What kind of path are you on? The idea of paths, roads, tracks, motorways, is an obvious metaphor for life because we have all experienced so many different real ones, from steep coastal paths to city roundabouts; we have gone down muddy lanes and crossed sandy, dusty ground where there really is no track to follow. Sunshine and rain, snow and heat, rocks, flowers, dry earth, all contribute to the conditions in which we travel. Some of us travel by day, others at night, when we may have artificial light, moon and starlight, or maybe nothing at all.

This exercise invites us to consider the path we are on, what it is like for us, and what that means for our spiritual path.

What you need

- Your imagination *or* a computer with internet access
- A journal or notebook
- Pen or pencil

The exercise

Find a place where you can be quiet and prayerful. Consider the question, 'What is the path of my life like right now?' What kind of 'place' is your life in? The reflection invites you to identify a particular kind of path that in some ways resonates with the circumstances of your life.

If you are searching your imagination, close your eyes and ask yourself, 'What is this path like?' Your deepest self will already have an answer, so do not analyse your circumstances, just let a picture form in your mind. It might surprise you.

Ask your imagination these questions:

- What is the ground like underfoot?
- What is around me?
- What is the weather like?
- Is it night or day?
- Can I see far ahead?
- Is the path wide or narrow, crooked or straight?
- Am I going uphill or down, or is it flat?
- Does this path have steps or other features?
- Is this a lane, a path, a road, maybe even a motorway?

Let the picture form in your mind and stay with it for a time.

Alternatively, if your imagination needs help, use the internet to find a selection of images using a search such as 'paths'. This will generate a vast range of possibilities. Scan through them and at some point you may find that one in particular jumps out at you, though you may not be sure why. Something resonates for you; there is an echo in the image of your experience, though you might not know right away what that is. Download this image if you can or isolate it on the screen, and have it before you so that you can engage with its message more deeply.

Now you have an image, either in your imagination or right in front of you, consider the following questions:

- What is it about this image that speaks to my experience?
- What is it like to be on this path?
- Does this image surprise me?
- What does it tell me that I did not know before?
- What emotions and sensations arise within me?
- How might I take this into prayer?

Further reflection

The power of this exercise is in the invitation to truly recognize and name where we are. If we are lost and unaware of our surroundings, we will never move forward. Naming the place we are in helps us to understand why we might be having particular feelings or reacting in certain ways. It may even open our eyes to why we have become ill or restless. Or we may deepen our sense of thanksgiving and wonder, and be reminded of gifts not to be taken for granted. Images of paths, roads and tracks may come to us in our dreams and it is important to pay attention to these because they emerge from our inner wisdom where the Spirit is at work to integrate and heal us. Our dreams sometimes present us with images that are surprising, even shocking; it is only when we explore them deeply that we become aware of unresolved questions and tensions. If you find a particular image arising in your dreams, take note of it and perhaps discuss it with a spiritual director or someone who will listen without trying to interpret it for you.

In a group

Ideally, provide a good number of postcard-sized images which you can spread out on the floor or on a table. You need to cover a wide range of images and have enough to give people a choice, even if someone else takes the picture one individual was drawn to. You might collect pictures over a period of time from cards or magazines. If the group is small you could just print off a selection – the cost would be prohibitive to do this for large numbers. Certain internet sites provide the images themselves free of charge that you can use without needing copyright permission.

Display your images and give the group members time to choose one, take it with them to a quiet place and spend time with it. Encourage the group to 'let the picture choose them', rather than try and think through logically what a good match might be. The picture that is 'the one' often has layers of encouragement, comfort, challenge or insight that were not initially obvious.

4

Roundabouts

One thing about roundabouts is that once you are on one you are forced to make a decision. Have you ever found yourself driving round a roundabout and concluding that none of the exits looks like the right one, so you repeat the process and go round again? As you sail round in a second or even a third attempt, you hope that no one notices your indecision, while also trying to ensure that your lane manoeuvres are not hazardous.

At some point you have to decide. There is a chance that you will pick an exit, travel 500 yards and then realize it was the wrong choice. Usually you can go back and try again, or correct your mistake another way even if it means doing an extra five miles. But life itself may not be so simple, and a choice once made might be irrevocable.

This reflection might help you consider complex choices and potential future routes. If you are thinking about a very specific choice, the exercise 'Which way?' is an alternative.

Whenever we have to make a life choice, we may dwell on both the future and the past, getting caught up in all the 'what ifs' of anxiety and regret. After we have taken a particular path, we may wonder what would have happened if we had picked another route. Of course, we cannot know the answer to this, because had we made that 'other' choice, a thousand variables would immediately come into play and every one of those variables would have presented yet more possibilities for delight or sorrow. The relationship or the job, the home or the trip, whatever we might have pursued could have numerous other twists and turns and endings; the road not taken is an illusion that has no existence. We must live with what is. We can make prayerful, informed, discerning and compassionate choices as far as we are able, then we must let the journey take us where it will.

What you need

- A large sheet of paper, at least A2
- Coloured pens

The exercise

Draw a circle in the middle of your paper, about the size of a dinner plate. Find one to draw around if you want to be neat. Now you are going to make your circle into a roundabout. Around your centre, draw some exits, perhaps three or four, representing different options that might be open to you at the moment. If you have more options and ideas than will easily fit, you might want to group your ideas and then repeat the exercise another day. So if, for example, you are considering teaching, or voluntary work, or further study, each of those might have more options attached, such as whether to teach children or adults, to work locally or overseas, to learn Japanese or DIY. Don't make it too complicated to begin with; save the sub-choices for later. Every exit leads to another roundabout sooner or later.

Now you have a roundabout with several exits. Start by considering the middle. What words would you like to use to describe being in this place of choice? They might be positive or negative, or a mixture, such as angry, bereaved, excited, gloomy, puzzled, gifted, amazed.

At each of your exits, add a sign and an arrow indicating where that road will take you. It doesn't matter if you have a spare exit, it might be useful later. As you consider each of these exits, write down some questions about what it might mean for you to make that choice. Your questions might be practical, such as 'Is it too far?', or spiritual, such as 'Is this really what I am called to do?'

Or possibly relationship issues will be to the fore: 'Will my family understand?' Note down all your questions but don't start to try to think of answers; just write down everything that occurs to you.

After a time you will feel that you have more or less got your ideas down. Sit back and just look. Ask yourself, 'What do I notice?' Do some options have a lot more writing around them than others? As you look again, is there anything you might learn about what seems to be important?

Notice your inner movements and change of mood as you look at each option and its questions for a few moments.

Now consider the following questions:

- Regardless of all practical considerations, other people, or life realities, which of these options makes my heart sing?
- Putting aside the sensible hat, which we do sometimes have to wear, which of these options feels 'heavy' to me?
- What else do I notice about the feelings attached to my options and questions?

A consideration of feelings does not mean that we should take the option that makes us feel happy, or avoid what might seem heavy or difficult. An exercise like this simply allows us to recognize and name those things so that any choices we decide on are made in the full light of awareness. For example, we might say that however sensible it may be, I cannot do that hard thing because I realize that eventually it would suck the life out of me. Or we might say that this is going to be hard, but it is the best way to go, and I can see ways of finding support and making this a fruitful time.

As you finish this exercise, consider the following questions.

- What do I need to do now?
- Is there information I need to obtain?
- Do I need to have a conversation with someone in particular?
- What is my next action?

Further reflection

Life requires so much of us that none of us can afford to be without our full attention. More often than we know, moments come that will make a difference to the quality of our lives. These are moments of choice that will never come again. They are moments of service, because others need our presence and attention, and moments of understanding in a world of much misunderstanding.[14]

In a group

This can be a good exercise to do in a group because people do the 'noticing' for each other; this can be very revealing and enlightening. Describe the exercise as above and give people time and space to go and work on their roundabout pictures. You should make it clear beforehand that participants will be invited to reflect in pairs.

After the pictures are complete, gather the group together and ask them to get into pairs. Ask each pair (A and B) to find a space and work together for 20 minutes. For the first 10 minutes, A

14 Kabir Helminski, *Living Presence*, Jeremy P. Tarcher, 1992, p. 34.

places their paper down without comment or explanation and B regards it with open and compassionate attention, not being too quick to speak. B then describes what they see, without interpretation, judgement or advice. For example, B might notice that one exit has a lot of questions; it would be helpful to say, 'There are a lot of questions there,' but do not add interpretation such as, 'You must be really worried about that.' If there is a really empty area on the drawing, B could offer, 'This looks quite open and empty in contrast with the rest of the paper,' but must resist suggesting, 'You clearly have not thought about this much.' The point about this is to notice and leave the 'owner' to wonder whether what has been noticed is of any significance. An empty space, or the choice of a particular word, could have many meanings. Notice, observe, describe, but don't draw conclusions or make judgements.

This first 10 minutes should be used in full. If B runs out of things to notice, the pair should sit in silence together to allow A to consider in silence what B has commented on. This silence may be important, so don't be tempted to engage in a discussion; this will only take you into unnecessary explanation. At the end of the 10 minutes A should merely say thank you and not feel obliged to explain further.

Then it is A's turn to look at B's picture in the same way. Again, use the 10 minutes to the full and allow silence if there is no more to be said. After 10 minutes, B says thank you to A and that part of the exercise is over.

Draw the group back together for a debrief, if you consider it appropriate. These few minutes could allow group members to say what they have learnt and to voice any emotions present. There is no need to describe everything that happened in the pairs, though some people may want to express what the experience was like or share a powerful insight, such as, 'I did not realize how excited I was until I was invited to see that the writing there was bigger.'

5

Invitation

This exercise is about the hopes and opportunities in our lives that excite, inspire and even thrill us. You can tell that it's a special invitation, for example, before you open the envelope because of the weight of the envelope, the feeling of thick card inside and maybe special decorative touches which suggest, 'I was made with care'. It is wonderful to open an invitation and see that you are asked to attend a very special event. You know it will be great fun, you will meet people you love, or interesting people you have never met before. There will be amazing food, beautiful music, in enchanting surroundings. Immediately you start to think about what you might wear, how you will get there, and you will soon be planning every detail in order to make sure that nothing can spoil the event.

God is at work in our lives, inviting us to all kinds of opportunities every day in quite ordinary ways. There may be a sense of invitation for something future too. Often when people test a vocation to ordained ministry, they speak of a sense of invitation going back many years. A seed was planted long ago, an idea that a call might come one day. When that day comes, how will we respond? An invitation comes with your name on it, it is intended for you, and perhaps others close to you, but it is very specific. You have been chosen to receive it, not anyone else.

Sometimes when we receive an invitation we have to weigh up how we are going to respond. Do I want to go? Will I have to change other plans? Can I get out of it? An invitation from God might be something we would change everything for.

The Sufi poet and mystic Rumi summed up the importance of a single-minded approach to vocation in this story:

The Master said; There is one thing in this world which must never be forgotten. If you were to forget everything else, but did not forget that, then there would be no cause to worry; whereas if you performed and remembered and did not forget every single thing, but forgot that one thing, then you would have done nothing whatsoever. It is just as if a king had sent you to carry out a specified task. You go and perform a hundred other tasks; but if you have not performed this one particular task on account of which you had gone to the country, it is as though you have performed nothing at all. So man has come into this world for a particular task, and that is his purpose; if he does not perform it, then he will have done nothing.[15]

It is important not to misunderstand this story as suggesting that God has a 'blueprint' for our lives that we must fulfil or else be condemned as failures. There is no 'destiny' against which we will be judged, for that would portray a harsh image of God indeed. The point is perhaps to underline in an uncompromising way the truth that there is something that you, and only you, can do. There is a wide open invitation to be all that we are called to be, in order to truly live.

What you need

- Stiff paper or card, about A5 size
- Pencil and ruler
- Scissors, or craft scissors for decorative edging
- Coloured pens – gold or silver ones would be ideal

---

15 'Discourses of Rumi', in Helminski, *Living Presence*, p. xii.

The exercise

Use the pencil, ruler and scissors to create a blank invitation card. You could make impressive wavy edges if you wish, and add a decorative border. These details are not significant in themselves, but they slow you down and enable you to become attentive and reflective. You could do this exercise on the back of an envelope if you wish, but you will not have given your imagination the opportunity to work, so try to take some time and care. While you are doing this, be aware of God's presence and expect God to speak to you.

Now hold your beautifully made, blank invitation in your hands and prayerfully consider what kind of invitation would really thrill you. Take plenty of time to hold this empty invitation and allow your heart to wonder about it. If God sent you an invitation that would inspire you, what might it say? You may have no idea to begin with, but as you sit and ponder, the Spirit will bring something to mind, and it might be a surprise.

When you are ready, write this invitation on the front of your card. Write your name, then underneath, 'You are invited to ...' and dare to express this deepest sense of call. Notice what is happening within you as you write these words and then look at them.

Allow some time to be with this invitation. Then turn the card over and write a 'reply' to God. What do you want to say to God in response? Be honest; God knows what is in your heart, so give it words.

Reflection

What is God's invitation to you? What would be the first thing that you would instantly say, without thinking about it? What might the deepest invitation of God be to you? When you allow the Spirit to offer a response, instinctively and unplanned, you may be amazed at what pops up. What response is deep within you?

Further reading

The book *Healing the Purpose of Your Life* explores the personal call that each person has from God, as a way of being truly and uniquely 'me'. It speaks of 'a special way of being that animates all our "doings". As we discover "how" we are meant to be in the world, "what" we are do with our energies and time unfolds from there.'[16]

In a group

Provide some pieces of card and plenty of pens or crayons to decorate them with, and perhaps craft scissors to cut fancy edges to the cards. Encourage each person to create a blank invitation and then spend time initially just holding this empty card in prayer. Let the group know that as they wait and listen, they will 'hear' the invitation and know what it is.

---

16 Dennis Linn, Sheila Fabricant Linn and Matthew Linn, *Healing the Purpose of Your Life*, Paulist Press, 1999, p. 2.

6

Jigsaw pieces

Some people love jigsaw puzzles, others just can't be bothered with them. Fitting things together can be enjoyably challenging, or just plain boring. We can choose to avoid boxed jigsaws, but the jigsaw of life is harder to put on one side. There are the pieces, spread out all over the place, making no sense whatsoever. Sometimes the task of making one picture from a lot of random bits of shape and colour seems impossible. Where do you start? What is your technique? Some begin with the edges, others with the mound of sky-coloured bits, others in one corner.

Life throws us a lot of things that can appear very disconnected and unrelated. In our work, or lack of it, we face a whole set of circumstances, unknowns, difficulties and joys. In another part of our life, relationships with family, friends, neighbours and worshipping community develop, grow, change, even enter periods of conflict or tension – and all this brings joy, celebration, worry and responsibility. We also have to deal with health, learning, finance, leisure, beliefs and skills. Life can be fast-paced, and fragmented, requiring us to relate to many people who may not connect with one another in any way. The result can be a sense of being overwhelmed, distracted and confused. It can seem as though different parts of our life conflict with one another, and things don't seem to come together. What is best for one person is not best for someone else, and not everyone can be kept happy all at the same time.

This is a reflection for those difficult fragmented times when things don't seem to fit together at all. It can be a real puzzle when there is a strong sense of call from God, but life does not seem to make it possible for you to follow it through. At such times we may question whether we have heard right, or whether God knows what God is doing. The exercise won't necessarily bring everything together right away, but naming the chaos is a good place to start. Chaos can be creative; in fact, some would say that chaos is necessary to creativity. When I was a child, before the school holidays arrived my mother would start collecting junk. There would be egg boxes, yoghurt pots, lids from a variety of containers and other containers without any lids, cereal boxes and washing-up liquid bottles. Then the whole lot would be tipped out in a heap on the floor and we would ask, 'What can this lot make?' Some things would prove useful, others were left for another day. The heap on the floor is not like a ready-made 'kit', with all the pieces numbered and lined up so that all we have to do is follow the instructions. Life is not usually like that. But with patient listening and a willingness to be surprised, new and unexpected things may become possible.

What you need

- Stiff paper or thin card
- Pencil, ruler and scissors
- Coloured pens
- A candle or tea light and some matches

The exercise

Find a place to be still and silent. Remember God's presence and ask for wisdom and hope, or whatever it is that you most need at this time. With a pen or pencil, draw some jigsaw puzzle pieces, each about postcard size so that they are big enough to write on, and cut them out. You might need about 10 or 12 of these, depending on what is happening in your life, so make plenty. You do not need to design your jigsaw pieces so that they fit together; the point is rather that you cannot see how they might join up. It might be tempting to shorten this exercise by just making a list

43

or thinking about the different aspects of your life. However, the activity of drawing, the cutting round your lines with scissors and the creation of your pieces is an important part of the reflection. This will slow you down, taking you into a reflective and open space. You may be surprised at the thoughts and emotions that arise as you simply cut round a jigsaw shape. Intentional activity is known to have spiritual benefits, as many artists or people who work with their hands will tell you.

Lay the pieces out on the floor or a table so you can see them all. Just notice what effect this has. Is there a sense of fragmentation in your life? Where do you feel it in your body? Now take some time to prayerfully reflect on all that seems fragmented and chaotic in life at the moment. Offer it to God and ask for help in acknowledging all the different pieces.

When you are ready, write one thing on each jigsaw piece: something that seems to be one of the bits that are not coming together in your life. There will be life-giving and challenging aspects to the puzzle. You might need to name things such as 'my child is ill' or 'my family are worried by my sense of call', alongside 'I want to travel' or 'I love my job'. Consider whatever is making up your sense of chaos; tease out the areas of stress, pressure or worry, as well as what is giving you life. Give each one a jigsaw piece of its own. Write, draw, use colour, add question marks, exclamation marks, stars or whatever expresses your sense of fragmentation.

Reflection

When you have finished, spread out the pieces and place the candle in the middle of them. As you light it, prayerfully commit all these fragments, circumstances and people to God. Open your hands to God, praying for whatever you need. Wait in the stillness for as long as you need to. Be open to receive the gift of a surprising or reassuring 'word' offering strength and hope.

Prayer

God, in the chaos and conflictedness of my life, in the fragmentation and dissonance, I know you are with me. I cannot see how these pieces fit together, and perhaps they never will. However, you do not need tidiness, order, predictability, and this mess is just the raw material of resurrection. I wait in stillness and darkness for you.

In a group

The group could cut out their own shapes, but if there is not time, prepare plenty to take with you. When everyone has written on some pieces, you could invite them to share in pairs some thoughts and feelings that have emerged.

Close with a prayerful reflection. For this you could take a jigsaw with lots of pieces, the more the better, and tip the pieces out on the floor or on a low table. Place a candle in the middle and use a prayer such as the one above. You could invite the group to bring their chaos to God as they place some or all of their own pieces around the candle. They can turn them over if they don't want their writing to be visible. Encourage participants to take their pieces away afterwards. If any are left, dispose of them appropriately.

7

Landscapes

What is the landscape of your life like? We often talk about our lives in metaphorical terms, whether it is the 'slough of despond' from Bunyan's *Pilgrim's Progress*, or the 'dark night of the soul' of St John of the Cross. We speak of 'mountain-top' experiences, or hope for 'the light at the end of the tunnel' or perhaps we pass through a 'valley of despair'. A whole generation was reduced to tears as Mother Superior in *The Sound of Music* gazed out of the convent window and sang to the troubled young nun, Maria, 'Climb every mountain, ford every stream, follow every rainbow ...' We speak of the weather and the seasons, as well as the terrain, and in Britain, while we do not have Saharan deserts or tropical rainforests, there is plenty of material for metaphor to be found across our landscape.

This reflection invites you to consider which landscape metaphors describe the journey you have been on throughout your life. You might have experienced sunny hillsides, bogs, rivers and waterfalls, deep woods, or snow-covered mountains; the possibilities are endless. When a metaphor comes to mind, it may bring with it 'value-added' meaning. For example, we may feel that an experience was like 'being in a blizzard' but the metaphor comes more from our intuition than from a logical search for an exact match for our mood. So when something within, apparently unprompted, gives us the word 'blizzard', we may find more layers to explore. Why did that come to mind? You might ponder the way that a blizzard can cover over familiar landmarks very quickly so that you become disoriented, and find that your experience does indeed echo something of that. A blizzard can sting your face and eyes, so that you need to protect yourself as best you can while still finding your way forward. A blizzard can prompt you to stop, seek shelter, and acknowledge that you will be in danger if you press forward. For a time, you are forced into the present moment and the world immediately around you.

Metaphors are rich, creative, instructive, fascinating and surprising. You can play with them as you consider the course of your life, noticing the patterns that arise when we think, 'Here I am again, I recognize this place.' We return to the same 'place' for various reasons; it can be a positive, healing refuge, or the result of not fully learning from a previous experience. It is fascinating to see how certain themes, choices and patterns turn up throughout our lives. What we experience and choose today may be a reworked version of previous choices; not a simple case of history repeating itself, if we have learnt and grown, but another trip round the loop to deepen and develop who we are. If you are a person who likes fresh starts and risks, or soon gets bored, you are likely to see this recurring – a fact which in itself is neither positive nor negative – but you might want to ask, 'What is going on? Is this a creative, seasonal renewal, or is it some kind of sticking point it would be good to move beyond?'

What you need

- A large sheet of paper, preferably flip-chart size
- Coloured pens

The exercise

Place your paper on the floor or table, 'portrait' style (with one short end towards you). Starting here (representing the point of your birth), begin to make a line across the paper, moving away from you, to represent your life journey. Don't make this a straight line; use the whole width of the paper too, so it could be a wavy line. This will give you space to add things along the length of the line – and in any case life is not a straight line at all.

The place where you put the end of the line represents where you are now.

Now begin to think about your life and what terrain you have passed through. Along the line, draw symbols, with a few words if you need them; use colour to represent the mountains and valleys, rivers and deserts, gardens and cities, marshes and woodlands. Be creative. Add weather if this is useful. Take plenty of time, drawing on your inner sense of how you experienced a place and being open to surprising metaphors.

This exercise really needs a couple of hours to allow time for memory and review. Don't 'attack' the task but approach it meditatively with lots of pauses to ponder. The important thing is not necessarily to finish, but to spend time understanding your experience more deeply.

When your line is about complete, just look at it for a while and ask:

- What patterns are clear to me?
- Were there times when I revisited the same 'place'?
- Was this a healthy, seasonal cycle, or did I repeat a previous 'mistake' (God recycles mistakes) a number of times, with the same kinds of consequences?
- What can I learn from this life map?
- What new insight has emerged from this exercise?
- Are there implications for future choices or ways of being?

You can find your life's poetry, words and images that express the contradictions and ironies that shape you. One of the simplest expressions of this mystery are the Irish knots and spirals, images that go back thousands of years, showing the complexities and circularities of every human life. Modern science prefers the straight line of evolution as the energetic principle. The Irish spirals complement the Taoist idea that a thing is always entangled with its opposite; yin always moving into yang.[17]

---

17 Thomas Moore, *Dark Nights of the Soul*, Hachette Digital, 2004, p. 306.

For a gently humorous reflection on learning from life's patterns, look up Portia Nelson's poem 'Autobiography in Five Short Chapters'.[18]

Reflection

Every landscape has its gifts and costs. We can learn and grow in both sunshine and shade, but in the valleys and deserts we have to work harder to find light and water to sustain us. There may be a gift for us in the most challenging of environments. George Matheson, who wrote the hymn 'O Love that wilt not let me go' out of the depths of his spiritual suffering, said:

> There are songs that can only be learnt in the valley. No art can teach them; no rules of voice can make them perfectly sung. Their music is in the heart. They are songs of memory, of personal experience. They bring out their burden from the shadow of the past; they mount on the wings of yesterday.[19]

In a group

This reflection requires plenty of time, so it is perhaps best suited for a residential retreat or workshop. It takes a couple of hours or so for people to 'plot' the outline of their journey and then begin to see themes and patterns emerge. It is important to have long enough to consider these cycles, otherwise you may have the narrative of the 'story' but this may seem more like a string of unconnected events rather than a tapestry of interconnecting threads, loops and recurring themes.

---

18 Neil Astley and Pamela Robertson-Pearce (eds), *Soul Food*, Bloodaxe, 2007, p. 43.

19 George Matheson, 'Streams in the Desert', in Gordon MacDonald, *Rebuilding Your Broken World*, Highland Books, revised 2004, p. 10.

8

Which way?

When a new possibility presents itself, is your first reaction to be optimistic or cautious? Some people think about all the plus factors first and believe everything will work out, while others are less positive about committing, perhaps because they want to protect people and things (though not necessarily merely material objects) that are important to them. This may not be simply a matter of 'faith'; our upbringing, personalities and previous experiences all play a part in how risk-averse we are. We may need both points of view so that options can be weighed up, or discerned. At the outset, the best possible outcome is no more than a hope, and the worst possible outcome 'might never happen'.

This reflection invites you to consider what taking a risk and going into an unknown future could look like, if it proved to be all that you hope and trust it could be. But if you are teetering on the brink, holding fears and anxieties for others as well as your-self, then this exercise may help you to assess whether those things are enough to stop you going forward, or whether there may be strategies to lessen the impact of the difficulties you may face.

What you need

- Two large sheets of paper
- Coloured marker pens

The exercise

Find a quiet space and still yourself with prayer, music or meditation. Offer this time of reflection to God, praying for inner honesty, courage and wisdom. Pray for those who may be affected by any life-changing discernment you may come to.

Now begin by considering the course of action or change you are contemplating. Notice your inner movements as you ponder what it would be like to take this step. Where in your body do you notice a response – perhaps joyful, perhaps anxious, maybe both?

Take your paper and pens. Imagine all the enticing possibilities associated with the path you are exploring. In what ways could this be life-enhancing for you and for others? What gifts might it bring you? What new dimensions could it add to your life? Dream of all the most exciting, liberating, life-giving things that could happen. Write these down on your paper. Include everything, however small. Describe the place you could be in by using the present tense, for example, 'I am loving living in the country', 'I am part of a team that really work well together', 'I see my grandchildren every day'. Paint a picture of the best scenario this could be. Fill the page; don't try to make a tidy list but fill the spaces on the paper as you go. Allow yourself to become hopeful, joyful and excited. If you notice pessimisms springing up, don't give them any attention right now – they can wait. Don't argue with them, just stay with the joy that is welling up in you. When you are done, notice how you feel and where you are experiencing the various sensations in your body.

Next, you need to put this sheet of paper out of sight. The reason for this is that as you come to consider your fears and forebodings, or just niggling concerns, you need to let them arise naturally and not as a mirror image of the positive possibilities. This could be a good moment to get a cup of tea or take a walk.

When you come back, take a few moments to return to thinking about the future and what it will mean. When you are ready, take a fresh sheet of paper and begin to note down the things that worry you. What are the worst possible outcomes for you and for others? These might be inner things such as 'I am bored', or quite practical things such as 'it's too expensive to travel to visit family'. Again, describe an imaginary present rather than just creating a list of potential pros and cons. This makes it more 'real' for you. By placing yourself in this scenario you are involving not just your mind as you think about this, but also your heart and your body, and they too have wisdom to offer.

When you have noted as many issues as you can think of, notice what feelings, thoughts and physical sensations are most present for you. Take enough time to really notice what is in you, and where in your body you carry any anxiety.

Now, take your two sheets of paper, place them side by side and offer them consciously to God. What do you notice about them? Just look and see what is before you. What do you notice about your hopeful thinking? What do you notice about your concerns and worries? What do you notice about where there is energy? What is happening in your body as you do this?

Reflection

Does this exercise shed any fresh light on your way forward? Remember that this is not simply about weighing up pros and cons but about being in touch with all that is hopeful and all that frightens you. Naming what we long for may help us to commit to it. Acknowledging our fears may shrink them away as we realize that they do not amount to much. Or it may be that in the light of all that is before us we come to a peaceful and trusting acceptance that now is not the time, and begin to move on rather than end-lessly churning and overthinking.

Sometimes we fall into the trap of believing that if we do the 'right' thing we will be blessed and protected, but if we do the 'wrong' thing we may fail, or invoke God's displeasure or even punishment. Then we need to review what kind of God we believe in, and whether we believe that life is a maze in which we have to figure out God's map. Such thinking can really keep a person awake at night. There are many possible paths in life, but God seems to be concerned only with where we are, that is all. How would you look at this if there was no 'right' way, if it was impossible to make a mistake, only a choice?

An exercise like this is just one way of beginning to get in touch with what change might mean for you. Discernment happens over a period of time. You may find it helpful to dwell on this for longer, perhaps on a quiet day or retreat.

Prayer

O God, my mind goes back and forth, this way and that, uncertain of the way ahead. I see possibility and I see risk. I want to trust you, and I have responsibilities that I take seriously too. Give me courage. Protect me from stupidity. May my caution not blind me to fresh horizons. May I not be overwhelmed by disproportionate fears and anxieties. You who are endlessly creative, weave your will and your way in me and with those I love.

In a group

As you draw the group together after this exercise you may wish to give them time to listen and share with each other, either in the group or in twos or threes. Try and encourage them to see this exercise as a discerning of the movement of the Spirit rather than a measuring of advantages and disadvantages. It is sometimes the case that even as we contemplate a course of action that is fraught with danger, joy draws us forward even though there is great risk involved. The right path is not always the sensible one.

9

Stepping stones

Children love stepping stones, and so do a lot of grown-ups. There is something uncertain enough to be exciting, while really being quite safe, about crossing a line of stones through water, especially if it is deep or running fast. You can see the other side before you start, but between you and the other bank it is wet and swirly and you might get water in your shoes, or worse, fall in altogether. But to leap and jump and safely make it, well, that can make you feel slightly clever and satisfied, and ready to do it all again.

Sometimes the stepping stones have been beautifully laid out, just the right distance apart, solid and flat. But sometimes they have not been placed there to help us at all, we just have to make our way across as best we can. The stones may be wobbly, far apart, or partly submerged. We can see the other side, but can we make it?

This reflection is about the stepping stones of life, the ones that we need to cross in order to reach another shore. There is danger, and we must weigh up whether to stay where we are, or fling ourselves into the crossing. It usually is a case of 'flinging' because tentative steps are more likely to land us in the water than quick and confident ones. Indecisive teetering could well be followed by a big splash as we fall in. This reflection is about finding the stepping stones and having the courage to walk on them.

What you need

- Several large sheets of paper or thin card
- Coloured pens
- Scissors

The exercise

With a pen, draw some large 'stepping stones' on paper or card. Each one should be big enough to write or draw on, at least A5 size. If you would like to actually step on your 'stones' and not just look at them, make them at least A4 size. Some people might find the physicality of standing on the 'stones' very helpful.

Cut out about a dozen, although you might not need them all. Find a space where there is room to lay out five or six of your stepping stones on the floor, arranging them just as you wish. Keep the rest on one side in case you want to add them later.

Now you don't do anything at all for a while! Just look at your stones on the floor and consider where you are now, and where it is you would like to get to, or wonder if you are being called to. Take plenty of time to just notice the thoughts and feelings and ideas that occur to you, but don't get hooked into plans, anxieties, or strategies or hopes. Just 'be' on this bank and notice everything. Absolutely do not try and solve any problems in your mind or ask 'how?' For now you simply need to be aware of the issues, questions and uncertainties that lie between you and the other side.

After a while, when you are ready, take some pens and start to write some words, or create a prayer, for each stepping stone. What might you need to overcome? What do you need from God or from others? Are there things you need to do? Is there something you are waiting for? Write each idea on a 'stone'. Add some more if you need to.

When you feel that you have got all your ideas down, take a look at your stepping stones and see if you want to rearrange them. Which ones should be nearest to you? These might represent something you can do quite easily or which might be resolved soon.

If you want to do something physical and you have the space, you could take a walk now across your stones. Notice what it feels like as you slowly step onto each one. Ask God for what you need at each stage. Be aware of what it is like to get to the other side. Alternatively, pick up each 'stone' and hold it while you commit to God all that it represents. Put it back in place with a prayer for courage and peace before taking the next one into your hands.

Further reflection

Try standing in different places: on this 'bank', the far side, and at various points across your stones. Consider:

- What is it like for me to be here?
- How did I get here?
- Where do I need to move next?
- What do I need in order to jump?
- What is holding me back?

In a group

This exercise needs a lot of space, unless you have only a very small group. It could work well outside, as long as the ground is reasonably dry and flat. When you gather the group together you could ask participants to share one step they plan to take next. A closing time of prayer could include silent or open prayer for others in the group, either generally or with an invitation to pray for those sitting next to you.

An alternative activity is to give each person a piece of flip-chart paper and invite them to draw a series of stones across it, writing or drawing in each one. This offers less flexibility and movement than cut-out 'stones', but it may be a more workable approach.

10

Voices

At times of change and uncertainty, we may listen for guidance, reassurance or wisdom. What we actually hear may be more like the sound of many conflicting voices in our heads. These voices may come from our faith, the Bible, our intuition, common sense, desire, reason. We may also be conscious of the voices of others: parents, children, friends, mentors, figures from our past such as teachers or authority figures. Every voice has something to say, some may appear helpful and encouraging, other voices seem to dismiss, warn, or even ridicule us. Have you had the experience of 'hearing' what a significant person would say to you, helpfully or otherwise, in a particular situation? 'I can hear her now,' we say. Children 'know' what their parents are going to say when they break the bad news of some misdemeanour, although they may be pleasantly surprised when the moment comes.

Bracelets carrying the words 'What would Jesus do?' have become popular as a daily reminder to check our instinctive reactions to people and situations, but what might it be like to have a 'What would Jesus say?' bracelet. It might be a huge gift – a constant turning to God's voice of encouragement or compassion. But if we were to assume, because of the idea of God that we carry around in our heads, that what Jesus might have to say is likely to be disapproving or judging, then that voice is not going to be very helpful. We need to recognize it as rooted in a distorted idea of God.

How can we know which voices are authentic? First we have to let them speak, then discern the extent to which we need to take note of them, how much attention to give them and what response is required. In the wilderness of temptation, Jesus struggled to reconcile the deep inner voice of a sense of vocation with the voices of temptation, which sounded smooth, credible, reasonable. For Jesus, it was the time in stillness and silence, listening to his own deepest sense of identity in God, that enabled him to resist the 'false' voices and have confidence in God's call to him.

This reflection creates a space in which we can identify the different voices calling to us, advising us, admonishing us, inspiring us. We can consider which voices are authentic, which speak the truth; we can then receive their wisdom. There may be voices too that we need to resist, sometimes with courage or humour.

What you need

- A large sheet of paper, preferably flip-chart size
- A blank postcard
- Coloured pens

The exercise

Take some time to be quiet and attentive to your inner world, and God's presence. Prayerfully ask for openness, honesty and discernment. As you consider your current circumstances, everything that is going on for you and the choices you may be considering, you may become aware of different 'voices'. Some messages may come from within yourself, such as 'you are just being silly' or 'it's your imagination' or 'they would never ordain someone like you'. Others may be what those people have actually said, such as 'brilliant' or 'that's a terrible idea'. Often they are things that we imagine those around us saying, even if sometimes we don't have any real evidence for this. These might include 'I hate that suggestion' or 'you are just stupid to entertain that plan'. Maybe what we 'hear' is people laughing at us. Spend some time now drawing speech bubbles on your sheet and write in them some of these comments. Use different colours, add pictures, such as little faces that express how these voices make you feel. Be honest about the voices you hear, what you tell yourself, and the things you believe others might say. Let the voices of the past have their say too.

Let all the voices you are aware of find expression. You do not have to show this to anyone, unless you choose to, so it is safe to give even the tiniest of whispers space. These might be things you really need to hear, such as 'you really can do this' or 'it will be all right' as well as 'be careful' or 'are you sure?'

When you are done, sit back and look at everything you have given a voice to. Take some time to ponder what is there and notice the thoughts, emotions and sensations the voices spark in you. As you consider these voices, ask yourself whether there are any that you can recognize as not authentic, but deceitful, misleading or distracting. It might be a voice from childhood, or something you have been taught about God. Notice these voices and see them for what they are. Do you really have to be guided by these voices, and should they have a place in your life? Next, notice if there are voices that strike you as being authentic, true and reliable, and most pertinent for you at this time. If none of the voices rings true for you, spend some time in silence and ask the Spirit to speak in a new way.

When you have some sense of an authentic voice, write the words you hear on a postcard. Fold up the big sheet and commit it to God in some way. Put it somewhere safe for later prayer and reflection, or you can destroy it. Take the postcard and sit with it for a while. Let those words sink into you with renewal, hope and healing. Put the card in your journal, Bible or somewhere where you will see it every day.

Reflection

Mary McAleese, President of Ireland from 1997 to 2011, described a conflict between the powerful voice of her Roman Catholic background, expressed not only by the Church but by her family and friends, and the voices in her head that began to question the teaching of the Church on the ordination of women to priestly ministry. She found it hard to listen to the voices of doubt, because she knew that many difficult and costly implications would ensue. Nevertheless, she came to recognize the authenticity of these 'voices', and found the courage and tenacity to trust them enough not to drown them out.

> To challenge the awesome authority of the hierarchy seemed to open an aptly named Pandora's box of things which might be difficult to swallow. If the Church was wrong, on an issue on which it spoke with a chilling clarity and certainty, then how many other errors might lie buried in that theology. There was a comfort in burying myself inside the group consciousness and putting my hands over my ears so that I could not hear the doubts that were running about in my head. To pit myself against the group meant challenging father, mother, family, parish, community and to live with some form of exclusion which, whether mild rebuke or subtle shunning, would surely follow.[20]

Have you had times of 'putting your hands over your ears'? How do you discern between the authentic voices and the false ones?

In a group

You could have quite a lively time of sharing around this. You could invite group members to share in the whole group, or with each other in twos or threes. The exercise could be effective as part of a day on pastoral awareness. People could speak about their own 'voices' or you could invite the group to consider Mary McAleese's experience and ask if there is any resonance here for them.

---

20 Mary McAleese, 'Reconciled Being, Love in Chaos: The John Main Seminar 1997', in Jeremy Young, *The Cost of Certainty*, DLT, 2004, p. 88.

11

Hot air balloon

I have never been as brave as a friend of mine who went on a pilgrimage to the desert. The group rode on camels to get there, slept under the stars and took only a few small things they could easily carry. It was an experience of being 'stripped back' and becoming exposed and vulnerable in every possible way, even if only for a few days. There are those who have gone into the wilderness to live. The desert fathers and mothers had very little to support or entertain them in their hermit existence, and although we are not all called to such an extreme lifestyle, they remain a sign and a challenge for us. It is sobering to consider just how many of the trappings of our lives we could do without if we really wanted to, or just plain had to.

Some people would have no difficulty going to an actual physical desert, while for others it would require heroic spiritual strength. Different people have a variety of needs and preferences. If you are interested in understanding what 'makes you tick', consider exploring the Enneagram – there are details about this in the Resources section at the end of this book. It can be helpful to see why some people find it easy to go to the 'desert' while others find it challenging.

I once went on a retreat near the sea, and I took long walks along the shore, often collecting attractive stones and pebbles, as I had done many times before. One day, feeling my pockets becoming heavier by the minute, I found myself wondering whether I really needed any more pebbles, and I had to stop and ask myself why exactly I thought I wanted them. Collecting stones can have a mesmerizing, addictive quality, and they always look so inviting when shiny with sea water.

For the rest of my walk, instead of continuing to fill up my pockets, I gradually emptied them, throwing the stones I had so carefully chosen one at a time into the sea. It was surprisingly difficult, not because I really needed them, but because I had chosen them and claimed them in some way and made them 'mine'. Nevertheless, by the end of the walk I had just one left, and although I did keep that one, I had experienced a sense of liberation. I held on to the last one because the call to be 'emptied out' does not require us to do violence to ourselves; it is an invitation that can liberate us, if and when we are able to respond freely.

Getting rid of 'stuff', whether in our outer world or our inner world, is not easy in the climate in which we live. 'Bargains' of every sort are under our noses every day; we can find anything we want on eBay and can shop without leaving our bedroom. This well-known syndrome of acquiring 'stuff', whether it is physical or virtual, rather ironically generates yet more 'clutter' in the way of books, TV programmes and magazine articles about decluttering. What a strange world we inhabit.

We collect inner and spiritual 'stuff' as well as the material sort. They are connected, of course, and contemporary hermits have occasionally described the stripping process of filtering the books and notes they have gathered over years, even in a simple life in religious community.

There are times when we need to jettison what we really no longer need. This may be old prejudices, images of God that no longer ring true, or theological perspectives that we have refined in the light of experience.

This reflection uses the metaphor of a hot air balloon, which in order to avoid crashing down into the bushes must throw anything that is not needed out of the basket, with no time to lose. In such life or death moments there is no agonizing, no struggle, everything must go.

What you need

- A large sheet of paper, preferably A2
- Coloured pens

The exercise

On your sheet of paper, draw a hot air balloon. Make it big enough to write in both the balloon and the basket sections. Take time to prayerfully centre yourself. In the balloon section write or draw things that express where you aspire to be as a person and as a disciple. This is not about job promotion or achievements, but who you are becoming through a process of inner growth. You might include something about your sense of vocation, or how you are living; focus on who you are rather than what you are doing. Don't hurry over this; allow a sense of your deepest potential to excite and challenge you.

Next, turn to the basket. Ask yourself:

- As I grow in my sense of God-given 'being', are there things I need to throw out?
- Do I have habits, compulsions, behaviours or attitudes that I am aware of but find it hard to let go of or change?
- Can I throw them out and change my priorities?

It has been said that if you do what you have always done, you will be what you've always been: a simple but true acknowledgement of how hard it is to let go of what we are attached to. The future is scary without the habits and beliefs that have always seemed reliable.

Finally, use some bright colours to draw the flame at the base of the balloon. Consider these points:

- What is my fuel?
- Where is my energy and fire?
- What gives me lift?
- How can I pray?

Further reflection

There might be many things we need to jettison: material posses-
sions, habits, addictions of various sorts, mistaken beliefs about
ourselves or others and, of course, ideas about God that may have
served us well enough in the past but now need to be reviewed
and refined.

The Jesuit priest and writer Gerard Hughes describes his experience of letting go of an attachment to a false idea of who God
was and what God wanted of him. As part of his work in a community, Gerard had begun to meet with a group of people in a
pub, where the discussion was often stimulating and lively well
into the night:

> Returning late from one of these meetings, I was struggling to
> complete the Divine Office, which every priest was bound to
> recite in full, omission of any one of the six parts being con-
> sidered a grave sin. Until then I had struggled through the Divine
> Office every day. That evening, with two parts unfinished, I put
> the book aside, feeling not guilty but free. It seems trivial, but
> for me it was a first step into freedom from the tyranny of exter-
> nal obligations.[21]

21 Gerard W. Hughes, *God, Where are You?* DLT, 1997, p. 111.

Cyprian Smith, writing about the mystic Meister Eckhart, describes the uncompromising challenge of Eckhart's teaching. We need to abandon any idea of God that in the end just gets in the way.

> Eckhart is very radical in the extent to which he wants us to be prepared to drop incomplete notions of God, however sanctified or traditional. He wants us to be prepared, when we are ready, to stop thinking of God as a 'Spirit' or as a 'Person' or as 'Father, Son and Holy Spirit'. There is a great deal of truth in these images; they are hallowed by the Church, and are, indeed part of God's own revelation of himself. Therefore they are to be respected and used as the Church commands; but not to be rested in, not to be considered as final, for though they are true images, the mere fact of their being images at all means that they contain an element of limitation and illusion. So when the Eye of the Heart opens, and the spiritual intellect takes flight towards the Transcendent God, all these images have to go. Eckhart will not let us keep a single one of them. Not only is God not wise or good, but he is not a Person either, not Trinity, not Father, Son or Holy Spirit. In the end, he is not even God, for Eckhart makes the prayer: 'therefore I pray God, that He may rid me of God'.[22]

What do you need to jettison?

---

22 Cyprian Smith, *The Way of Paradox*, DLT, 2004, p. 40.

12

What is your name?

Names are very important. Parents usually take great care (sometimes with interesting results) over choosing the names of their children. We can react strongly to being called names we don't like, nicknames and abbreviations that seem to mess with our sense of identity and label us in ways we don't find truthful or flattering. The difference between Pat and Patricia, Ann and Anne, Julie and Juliet, Robert and Rob, is not just a letter or two, it is the whole sense of who we are and how we inhabit the world. We are not someone else. Sometimes people change their names, legally or otherwise. I once heard of a retreat at which participants chose a name (any name at all) before they arrived and this would be how they were known during that time. Imagine being with a large group of people, none of whom have ever known your 'real' name, and they all call you by a name you may have only just invented for yourself. To you it sounds novel, but to others, as far as they are concerned, that really is your name. That could be a very interesting experience.

Names are tied up not only with the person they belong to, but also with the person who speaks your name. Who are they? Do they speak tenderly or angrily, accusingly or encouragingly?

The people who use our names are important in our lives. There is a naming that happens between each of us and God. We have many names for God, and God may have many names for us too, as God speaks and calls to us at different times and in different ways.

This exercise begins with a reflection on the names we have for God, allowing us to imagine the way in which God may be speaking to us in some particular voice today. Are we conscious of being in the presence of God who encourages, nudges, provokes, inspires, puzzles, forgives? Of course, all these are always true, and much more, but at particular times we hear God in different ways. God thunders, whispers, sings and teases. This reflection is partly about the many images of God we have. You are invited to be aware of the presence of God who speaks from a particular quality, and then to hear how this God names us and calls us. Every name is a call or a promise, an invitation to live in the fullness and possibility of that name.

What you need

- Your journal or notebook, or some paper
- Pen or pencil

The exercise

Read through the whole of this section and then put the book aside, so that you can close your eyes and take all the time you need to pray through this meditation. You need to be somewhere quiet and still. You might like to light a candle, listen to some music, and gently become aware of God's presence and become centred. This meditation might also be done while out walking, since movement suits some people better than sitting still. Think about the best environment to enable you to be centred rather than distracted.

Begin by simply allowing your mind to remember as many names for God and ways of describing God as you can. These are likely to come from Scripture, hymns and songs, metaphors from nature, poetry and your imagination. Just notice as many as you can without holding on to any one in particular. 'God' will include any way at all you think of God, including Jesus, the Holy Spirit, and abstract concepts such as 'fire' or 'light', as well as qualities such as 'compassion' or 'power'. Take a good while to simply notice the vastness of 'God' and the many ways in which we seek to name God. After a time, allow your mind to be drawn to one particular word, name or image. This may not be something you normally use in prayer; it might even be a surprise that you are focusing on this aspect of God today. Whatever it is, let other ideas drop away and be conscious of the presence of God who is named and described in this way. Engage with all the implications. If your word is 'love', allow yourself to receive that love. If it is 'fire', feel the heat of it, contemplate it in its fieriness and and all that means. Be with this name, this image, this aspect of God-ness.

Immersed in the presence of this God, now gently become aware of how this God names you. If you listen within and pay quiet attention without impatience or anxiety, you will know how God calls you by name today. It may be your own name that you 'hear', or some other word that expresses your relationship with God and God's love for you. It may be something quite surprising. Allow yourself to receive this name and hear it.

Take some time to be in the presence of God who names you in this way and calls you with this word. Write about it in your journal.

Further reflection

Look at these Bible readings:

- John 20.11–18, especially noting verse 16 in which Jesus simply addresses Mary by her name. Take some time to imagine the scene and put yourself in Mary's place. What is contained in Jesus' naming of Mary?
- John 1.42 and Matthew 16.13–20. Jesus gives Simon a new name, Peter, which is a sign of his vocation. Are you being invited to respond to a new name?

13

Poured out

Jugs are functional items, like plates, bowls and teapots. They may be very ordinary, or very beautiful, but the most important thing is that they have a job to do. A teapot that looks like a postbox, a cat, or a house may be quite pretty but will it do the job? A teapot is for making tea, and a jug is for pouring liquid out, or at the very least, containing it. The combination of form and function has resulted in some very beautiful examples, perhaps because jugs have a certain capacity for holding something, perhaps something precious, until needed. When these contents are required, the jug must be able to pour out, smoothly and efficiently. It can be really annoying to have to use a jug that is a 'bad pourer' due to either design or damage. If the proportions are not right, and the jug not well made, the result will be milk or custard all over the table.

This reflection starts with some very ordinary, perhaps quite functional items and invites us to use them as a springboard for thinking about our purpose, vocation, and especially our capacity for serving, living, self-giving, pouring out.

What you need

If possible, collect as many different kinds of jug as you can find around you. You might have a few in your kitchen and perhaps some more ornamental ones. You could also include other items that 'pour', such as teapots, watering cans, saucepans and so on.

You will need some paper or your journal or notebook, and a pen or pencil.

The exercise

Gather the jugs or similar items you have collected from around your home. Spread them out on a table or on the floor. Take some time to be still and look at what you have. Consider where each one came from, whether you like it or not, why you kept it, what you use it for. Then, as you prayerfully reflect, allow yourself to be drawn to one in particular. It may not be your favourite, it may not be special in any way, but you will find that one will seem to ask for your attention, something is resonating for you. When you have this sense of being drawn, pick up this jug and hold it in your hands for a while. Look at it from every angle, see how it feels, notice everything about it.

Then gently allow the following questions to present themselves:

- What does it feel like for me to be drawn to this jug?
- What drew my attention?
- Was I drawn by something visual, or by a memory or association?
- What does this jug do?
- Consider whether this jug is large or small, pretty or plain, strong or fragile.

- Is this item very valuable, or might it be thrown away some-time soon?
- Notice any chips, marks, scratches, and consider whether they have ruined it.
- What can it be used for? Can it hold water?
- Reflect on who this item might have belonged to previously and what it held.
- Who has been served by this and in what ways?
- How does this jug challenge me?
- In what ways might I be called to be like this?

Write in your journal or notebook about the sense of call you experience. If you were the kind of 'jug' you feel called to be, what words would describe you? Write a prayer asking for the gift and grace of the Holy Spirit to be the kind of vessel you are called to be.

Reflection

I have a favourite large jug I bought in a secondhand shop. It is the old-fashioned sort that used to be placed on a washstand before the days of plumbing. It was once plain white, but someone has decorated it with an additional flower border, which eventually started to flake off, having been added on top of the original glaze. I sometimes wonder who added this border and why. Was a plain white jug not beautiful enough? It had been finished, glazed and completed the way originally intended. Was it necessary to add more decoration?

Thomas Moore says this:

One of the most altruistic things you can do is be a good neighbour and an involved citizen. The soul is fulfilled by the ordinary. If you know people of high accomplishment, you may have noticed how they treasure the ordinary life, and how that life serves as a base for their more visible activity. Something highly spiritual in you may wish for wondrous success, but the deep soul longs for ordinary connection and engagement. It wants friendship and community. It longs for simple pleasures, and from its perspective, the idea of justifying your existence is a dangerous distraction.[23]

In a group

This exercise works well in a group because you could ask people to bring along a few jugs so you will have plenty to display. It is also quite a fun exercise which can get people talking and laughing and therefore could be used to change the pace between more serious activities. Be alert, though, to the possibility of profound contributions. The simplest of everyday items can unlock something and take a person by surprise.

---

23 Moore, *Dark Nights of the Soul*, p. 299.

14

Moment of grace

When we are aware of the abundance of life, synchronous events unfold in the continuum of time; love brings together what needs to be brought together.[24]

Have you ever had a moment when you knew you were, for some reason, in exactly the right place at the right time, somehow doing the right thing with the right people? We don't usually plan such moments; they come as gifts, sometimes out of nowhere. Suddenly, or perhaps afterwards, you have a deep sense of 'God-incidence' or 'kairos' moment, a mysterious yet graced coming together.

One aspect of vocation is being available to be in the right place at the right time, ready to be present, to speak, to listen, to act. When we are truly present and attentive, we may be more open to subtle indications that we might need to change our plans or do something unexpected. This is discernment, awareness, 'presence'. But we can be misled by an unconscious need to be needed, or too great a sense of our own importance, feeding our own agendas. It is a fine art to be present in a free way, that is not about 'me' at all. The only way through this minefield is deep, humble self-knowledge, true and unromantic compassion, and a willingness to trust our God-given intuitions and inner promptings.

This reflection invites you to ponder such instances and to consider how to be open to them, not as unusual but always surprising – yet not surprising at all – ways of encountering God, other people and events. Spiritual writer Eckhart Tolle describes how resistance or negativity is like closing the shutters of our life so that 'sunlight cannot come in'. Rather,

---

24 Helminski, *Living Presence*, p. 167.

When you yield internally, when you surrender, a new dimension of consciousness opens up. If action is possible or necessary, your action will be in alignment ... Circumstances and people then become helpful. Co-incidences happen.[25]

What you need

- Your journal or a notebook, or some paper
- Pen or pencil

The exercise

Take time to be still. Enter into a prayerful space by sitting somewhere quiet; or, if you prefer, go for a walk or get involved in something creative. Allow your mind to range over memories and relationships and consider the times and places where 'God-incidences' happened. What took place? Who was involved? What was the outcome?

Consider what you learnt from these graced moments. What stops me being 'present' to the circumstances, people and situations right where I am?

You may be reminded too of times when you were given an incredible gift, the gift of someone who called you, or turned up, at the most remarkable moment. Whatever language we choose to describe these gifts, it seems clear that they do not simply happen 'by accident'.

Are you ready to be a gift for someone else?

Further reflection

Difficult theological questions arise when we think about guidance and how it was that we came to be in the 'right place' at the 'right time'. After a tragedy, you may hear people speak of how they avoided being caught up in the events because they stayed at

---

25 Eckhart Tolle, *A New Earth*, Penguin, 2005, p. 57.

home or were held up, or made an apparently insignificant decision which altered where they were. They may feel that they were guided or protected in some way, a perspective that raises many questions about who we believe God is, how we understand God to be at work in the world, and whether we can meaningfully pray for guidance and protection for ourselves and those we love. The 'wise men' who visited the infant Jesus were 'warned in a dream'[26] to return home another way and avoid Herod. It is not unusual to hear people speak of a sense that they should go to, or avoid, certain people or places, with remarkable outcomes. This is a mystery, but what is certain is that the more we are present to the moment of 'now', the more available we are to the subtle connections and communications that link and bind people, whether we know it or not.

We are all connected in ways that are not fully understood, yet are acknowledged in modern science. It is possible for us to know more than we know, without knowing how. A mother's heart skips a beat when her daughter many miles away goes into labour. We know we must call a friend we have not seen for a while and we learn that they are facing great difficulty. Sometimes we know we have to act, be somewhere, call someone. Some people will see this as direct guidance from the Spirit of God, others put it down to the God-given spiritual connections that all human beings have, while others want to take God out of the equation altogether. Whatever our theology and science, we are all invited to be more deeply present and in that attentive presence we will hear and know more than we ever thought possible.

In a group

Introduce the theme with a few words about the experience of being in the right place and time. Invite members of the group to share in twos and threes, or in the whole group, depending on the context. Ask the group to reflect on what their experience means for a sense of vocation.

26 Matthew 2.12.

15

Space and place

Space and place are very important in our spiritual life and growth. We are physical beings, and the physicality of place can be very significant for us. You may have powerful memories associated with particular places of encounter with God. There is a strong Celtic tradition of journeying to one's place of resurrection. Stories are told of how the saints travelled to their destination, and having arrived and offered up prayers, died a natural and peaceful death willingly and voluntarily, apparently without sickness or warning, yet knowing that their days were over. The Celtic tradition speaks too of 'thin places' often in boundary lands such as mountains and coastlines, characterized by wild space, exposure to the elements and little if any material comfort or human company.

What you need

- A large sheet of paper, preferably A2
- Coloured pens

The exercise

Where are your places of encounter, your 'thin places' or locations of significant spiritual experience? They may not be places with any religious or spiritual associations at all – a coffee shop can be a place of revelation as well as a church.

On your paper, record in words or pictures some of the places that have been formational for you, or where you had a particular encounter with God. How have these encounters inspired, shaped or challenged you? Do you need to revisit the place and the 'conversation' to hear again what you heard then?

Further reflection

We may want to revisit certain places we have been to because they will renew something within us. Other places may have been formational for us at a particular moment, yet to return there would be to try and turn back time; these places have in fact already gifted us in the way we needed. Returning to such places can be nostalgic but not necessarily energizing in a new way.

Writing about Celtic Christian communities, Ian Bradley reminds us of the difference between tourism and pilgrimage, describing the 'growing market for spiritual tourism which is focused more on visiting particular places to gain a spiritual high than on cultivating a lifelong spirit of exile and finding one's desert place of resurrection'.[27]

Particular places – such as Iona or Lindisfarne, for example – can become 'thin places' for us, where we have had a significant experience of God, but we are called to come away again renewed for the continuing journey in our own place. We can look for inspiration, but we should not expect magic, nor are these resting places destinations in themselves.

In the monastic tradition, there is emphasis on stability, and spiritual value in staying put and allowing the place where one is already located to become the 'thin place', rather than seeking God in some other place.

Does my experience of encountering God in different places enable me to experience God in the place where I live and work?

---

27 Ian Bradley, *Colonies of Heaven*, DLT, 2000, p. 216.

In a group

Invite the group to share their experience of 'place', especially those that are unusual or surprising.

16

Roots and branches

I remember being amazed when I learnt as a child that trees grow as far underground as they do above ground. The thought of the roots of a huge tree, deep under the earth, reaching far and wide, was fascinating. I could see immediately that it made sense. How else would a tree survive, or be balanced enough not to fall over at the first hint of stormy weather? I grasped the concept of balance between whatever was visible and what would be needed out of sight to take the strain when gales came along. I could also see that the more leaves and fruit, the more structure would be needed to supply food and water, and the underground search would need to go ever further and deeper.

The principle that gives the tree life and keeps it stable and fruitful is a good one for our life too. The more we grow, stretch out, and become fruitful, the greater our need for deep roots will be. This reflection is an invitation to consider the balance between what is 'above ground' and the depth of our roots. The giving out in our lives and the sustaining factors need to be in harmonious balance. This is especially true at times of change, recalibration, or following a fresh sense of call to a new challenge. We can be nourished by spiritual disciplines, a worshipping community, perhaps a Rule of Life, as well as people (past and present), places, and life-giving activities. Wonderfully too, the things that sustain us are sometimes surprising and not of our own choosing.

What you need

- A large sheet of paper, the bigger the better
- Coloured pens

The exercise

Starting halfway up your paper, draw the outline of a tree trunk, adding a network of branches. Mirror this with a network of roots underneath.

Take some time to be still and quiet. Then start to write on the branches of your tree those things that require your energy, time, gifts, love, patience, and so on. You do not have to fill in one branch at a time too neatly, just write in and among them. It is the general idea that is important and you don't need to be distracted by trying to be too precise. You could draw fruits on the tree representing the things that you have invested in and given your energy to: your family, work, achievements and projects. Name everything that occurs to you, including the things that have not gone well or even seemed disastrous; they are still the 'fruits' of your experience.

When you have completed as much as you possibly can, including both big and tiny concerns, responsibilities, relationships and work, leisure and learning, stop and take a good look at your picture. If you are very creative, add colour, and draw in leaves and fruit, if this is meaningful to you.

Notice now the thoughts, feelings and emotions that flow through you, in particular any areas in which you feel energized, and those which evoke heaviness or a sense of being drained. Notice all this without judging yourself in any way. Do not rush this stage, but allow the impact of all the growth, energy, relationships and life to become very present and immediate to you.

After a while, when you are ready, begin to consider the roots. Start to write along them everything that has nourished you in the past and what sustains you now. Again, use this part of the page freely without trying to be too particular about each 'root'.

What gives you life, nurtures, energizes and renews you? Include not only the things that seem big, such as 'my family' but smaller representative details and examples, such as 'taking my daughter to school' or 'the woodpecker I saw this morning'. You might have special memories, for example a book you once read that has stayed with you. Do not edit your ideas but let your memory and imagination offer you a rich banquet of life's gifts. Include all the people and experiences that have contributed in one way or another to your capacity to be who you are today, with all that you are able to give and to be and to do.

Again, when you have done this, take time to look at your 'roots'. What do you notice about them? Are there people or circumstances you were reluctant to name but who or which have actually helped shape you? People say that what doesn't kill you makes you stronger. Where has adversity given you strength?

Then spend some time looking at the whole picture. Does it appear balanced? Are there areas above ground that are not fed by anything at all? Are there areas of deep inner life that don't find any outward expression?

Reflection

Ponder these words from Verena Schiller as you prayerfully reflect on what sustains you now, what has rooted you, whether you chose it or not, and how the grace of God comes not only through our roots but also from God's provision in sunlight and rain, day by day. Give thanks for those God has blessed through you and for the fact that you may know nothing at all about it.

A life of faith longs to be open to the Spirit, to be guided and sustained by God, to make real the imprint of the living Christ as the Way and the Truth. The cloth of life is woven of the same essential threads for all of us but the contexts vary enormously and for each one is unique. More often than not there is little we can do to alter the givens of our circumstances, yet our roots and our environment, even our genes, never completely decide our destiny.[28]

In a group

This reflection needs little if any adaptation for group use. You could display some suitable pictures, and use Bible readings and simple liturgy if you wish to lengthen the session, or use this as part of a quiet day.

28 Verena Schiller, *A Simplified Life*, Canterbury Press, 2010, p. 10.

17

Push and pull

When we are thinking about change, it is important to distinguish between the pushes and the pulls. Some things in our lives frustrate us, or cause difficulty, pain, conflict or just plain boredom. We can find ourselves groaning, 'I wish it wasn't like this' or 'I wish I was anywhere but here'. We start to cast around for alternatives, or escape routes. Dissatisfaction with our lot can be an appropriate prompt, motivating us to think about possibilities we never would have considered. Things we had thought beyond our experience, competence or capability suddenly stretch our imagination to the point where we might consider new risks and ponder whether perhaps, with the right support, training and resources, we could achieve them. Sometimes we need a little nudge before we look outside our comfortable rut.

On the other hand, considering new ventures just because we are not entirely happy may not be a good thing, but more of an unsettling distraction. There are times to dig deep, stay put and draw on values such as stability, faithfulness, perseverance, and even that difficult one, 'obedience', a word that belongs in the context of loving faithfulness but has nothing to do with the 'oughts' and 'shoulds' we are better off without.

So how can we know whether the idea of 'pastures new' is a matter of call or simply a case of the grass being greener on the other side? This exercise helps you to consider not only what is pushing you out and away, but also what may be singing and calling to you from some potential future life.

As well as things that make us want to leave, move on, get out, others may be calling us out, and on, and up. We may be enabled to say, 'I would love to ...' or 'Wouldn't it be great if I could ...' or 'I've always wanted to ... or even, 'That would be my dream job'. Confidence begins to spark if we say, 'Well, I never would have thought this possible, but ...' or 'I never dreamed this could come my way'.

The irritations that make us want to leave where we are can be part of a call, or maybe simply reveal a resistance to sticking with the call we have. What we hear singing to us from some other place can be of the Spirit, calling us to new music; or they can be fantasies that distract and even disable us from the here and now. It is really hard to carry on doing what you are doing if you are thinking about doing something else. Vocation has to be lived in the place where we are, and the people and circumstances present to 'today', and therefore any wonderings about the future can only spring from, be nourished by, and return to that place, the place where we are.

So we need to discern whether the discomfort and dissonance are calling us to go deeper into where we are or are nudging us to take courage for a new step. At the same time, we must prayerfully and honestly consider whether the sparkly new things over the horizon are the stuff of either mirage and illusion, or of true vocation.

How can you tell? A real sense of vocation may have elements of both push and pull. Or it may be all pull and no apparent push, in which case there may be an element of sacrifice. Or it might be all push and no immediate clarity about the pull, and that can feel like saying a prayer and then jumping off a cliff.

Here is an exercise to help you at least map out the push and pull factors. You will probably need to talk them over at some point with a spiritual director or other soul friend or guide, but a mapping exercise like this will help marshall your thoughts. As with all reflective exercises, do not edit or discount anything at all that pops into your mind. Be honest and get it down on paper, however surprising or uncomfortable it might be.

What you need

- A large sheet of paper, preferably flip-chart size
- Coloured pens

The exercise

On your piece of paper draw a vertical dotted line to create two columns. You might find as you go along that your columns flow into each other, so don't separate them with harsh dividing lines. Everything is connected, everything is related to everything else and although lines and boxes can help clarify our thinking, sometimes we need to let things run into each other a bit, as is the way in real life.

At the top of your paper, write 'PUSH' on one side. Make a list here of all the things that are giving you a sense of being pushed forward, upward or outward. These may be very positive things such as 'I have completed what I set out to do', or less comfortable circumstances such as 'there is constant tension with my employers'. They might simply be practical things, such as 'it's too far to travel every day now'.

When you have got a number of things down, write 'PULL' on the other side of the paper. List here what you feel is drawing you away, onward, the things you might be going towards rather than away from. These might include opportunities or passions; such as 'I want to learn a new language', or it might be work possibilities, family circumstances or a sense of vocation. Include everything that comes to mind even if it does not seem relevant; even name all your wild ideas, such as 'I would love to visit India' or 'I want to learn about pig keeping'. You may have no way of knowing how this might be possible but you are opening up a future that has a different shape and it begins with dreaming and wondering. You might never get to India, or keep pigs, but you might end up somewhere else you would never have travelled to unless you had played with ideas like this.

After a while you are likely to have all sorts of things on your paper. Take time to notice what is there and what some of your feelings are. Take a thick pen and circle anything that seems to have a lot of energy around it. For example, you might be in conversation with someone about new possibilities, and those conversations always leave you energized and hopeful. Or maybe the sense that it is time to move on has become overwhelming.

You now have a sort of map in front of you that contains a lot of information about where you are, where you might perhaps go – or at least what parts of it might look like – and you have made some distinction between the most important factors in your discernment and other things that make up the picture but might not be decisive.

Stay prayerfully with your paper for a while. You might like to discuss it with someone you trust – a friend or partner, spiritual director or minister. Or, having written all these things down you may simply wish to fold up your paper, put it somewhere safe and let it marinate for a few weeks or months. Sometimes change begins to simmer long before it is time to act, but our hearts are being prepared. We may need to make gentle suggestions to those around us so that they too have time to consider where the Spirit may be leading.

Further reflection

Helen Macdonald describes how, grief-stricken after the loss of her father, she decided to train a goshawk. The seeds were sown many years earlier when, helping at a bird of prey centre, she witnessed the release of a goshawk. This might be seen as a 'pull' for her, at an early point in her life, long before it would be realized.

> She opened her wings and in a second was gone. She disappeared over a hedge slant-wise into nothing. It was as if she'd found a rent in the damp Gloucestershire air and slipped through it.

That was the moment I kept replaying, over and over. That was the recurring dream. From then on the hawk was inevitable.[29]

Later, in the midst of her shattering bereavement and only able to exist in the immediacy of the present moment with all its drive and compulsion, Helen is training her own hawk:

> *I can't go to Berlin in December*, I'd thought, appalled. *I have a hawk to fly*. Ambitions, life plans: these were for other people. I could no more imagine the future than a hawk could. I didn't need a career. I didn't want one.[30]

Interestingly, it seems that there was no push or pull here for Helen, either out of her place or towards the future; she was pulled completely into the present. What she found was that perspectives that might, in another time and place, have been taken for granted (the offer of prestigious work) suddenly have no currency at all.

29 Macdonald, *H is for Hawk*, p. 19.
30 Macdonald, *H is for Hawk*, p.123.

In a group

Introduce the exercise with a short talk about the way we experience push and pull factors, using the description at the start of this
section, or in your own words. Give members of the group large
sheets of paper and some pens. Invite them to spend some time in
silence identifying as many push and pull factors as they can think
of, encouraging honesty so that people do not filter or judge their
ideas. It may be important to say that they will not have to show
their paper to anyone later, unless they choose to do so; they do
not need to be concerned about what others will think.

Give the group at least half an hour, then draw them back
together. At this point, invite people to take 10 further minutes
on their own to consider where the 'energy' is on their paper. This
might be negative ('I hate my job with a passion') or positive ('I
dream about skydiving every night and I now have 117 books
about it').

18

Shoes

Shoes are such everyday items, but range from the purely functional to the highly decorative, possibly uncomfortable or even damaging. In some parts of the world it is normal to own several pairs, if not many, and it is hardly surprising that they turn up as a figure of speech in such sayings as 'if I were in her shoes' or 'now the boot is on the other foot' as well as in songs like 'These boots were made for walking'. Shoes represent so much to us, and the ones we choose to own and wear the most often might say quite a lot about our lives. They are very personal items, the best ones softening, shaping and stretching to fit our feet perfectly. Shoes are certainly not just about what to put on our feet so we can walk from here to there. There is a sad incident in Thomas Hardy's *Tess of the d'Urbervilles* where Tess loses her precious everyday boots, having hidden them in a hedge. She had changed into a pretty but impractical pair to try to give a better impression so that she could plead for help at the door of the family who might take pity on her. But the plan fails, and when her hidden boots are discovered, she is too humiliated to claim them. Bootless, her desperation can only deepen, and this moment is a significant turning point in her unfolding tragedy. Shoes can save your life.

This exercise is an invitation to consider where your 'shoes' might take you in life. Reflecting on a pair of shoes might be a surprising prompt into prayer about where your path is heading, who is with you, what kind of shoes you might need in the future. Do you have the right shoes for your journey?

What you need

- A pair of shoes, either ones you wear a lot or ones that are special to you in some way
- Your journal or notebook and pen or pencil

The exercise

Choose a pair of shoes to take into your prayer reflection. New or old, well worn or hardly used, functional or dressy, go with whatever seems to be drawing you. They might be a favourite pair, or maybe a pair you never wear, or even some you don't like or that are painful to wear.

Put the shoes on the floor or on a surface close to you. Look at them for a while, then pick them up and feel their weight and texture. Without forcing anything, let the following questions arise gently:

- When did I last wear these?
- Do I love them or hate them?
- What were my hopes and expectations for them when I first had them?
- What do they represent for me?
- Where have I worn these?
- Where do I expect to wear them again?
- Do these shoes 'fit' me?

Prayerfully consider what these shoes suggest about your journey, memories, sense of vocation and future hopes. What place do they have in your life now? What kind of context are they really made for? Are you going there?

Write in your journal or notebook what you have learnt during this prayer time. Have you had fresh insights about the shoes you have or the shoes you need?

In prayer, ask:

- Maybe I need a different pair of shoes altogether. What do I really need?
- If God gave me a pair of shoes, what might they be like?

Further reflection

This exercise is about shoes, but you might also like to consider what it is like not to wear shoes at all. Sometimes people choose to go barefoot as a sign of poverty and humility. People in some religious orders either go barefoot or wear the simplest possible sandals. The word 'discalced' means 'without shoes', and the order of the Discalced Carmelites was founded by St John of the Cross, who felt that existing religious orders had become too soft and corrupt. He called his followers back to a more austere and authentic way of life, as a sign of being totally focused on God, free from distracting and corrupt desires and ambitions.

Going barefoot is also a sign and an experience of being close to the earth, allowing our bodies to make contact with the ground beneath our feet. When do you cast away your shoes and what effect does it have? Consider these words from *The Prophet* by Kahlil Gibran: 'the breath of life is in the sunlight and the hand of life is in the wind ... forget not that the earth delights to feel your bare feet and the wind longs to play with your hair'.[31]

Our world is often too dangerous a place to walk barefoot, because we have damaged and polluted the ground so much. Are there places in your life where your feet can touch the ground and you need no shoes?

In a group

This would not be a very easy reflection to do in a group without considerable adaptation, since people do not generally wish to remove their shoes in public without being warned. The best way to do it would be to ask people to bring a pair of shoes to the session. Or you could lead a meditation in which people are invited to think of a pair of shoes they own, and include the questions above in the meditation. Alternatively you could provide a

---

31 Kahlil Gibran, 'On Clothes', *The Prophet*, Oneworld Publications, 1998.

good number of pictures of a variety of shoes and invite members of the group to choose one, spend some time with it and then reflect with one another. Another idea is to take along some pairs of shoes yourself, perhaps collected from charity shops.

You could close with some prayers about vocation and ministry. Include some intercession too, for religious orders and all those who, for so many reasons, have no shoes.

19

Traffic lights

When we are driving, traffic lights are essential for safety and order. They tell us when it is safe to go, and they indicate in no uncertain terms when the right thing to do is to stop where we are, or we will put ourselves and others in danger. They also warn us that we will be required to stop in a moment, if we have not already done so, and they gently invite us to 'get ready' as the time for movement approaches.

This reflection invites us to think about life's traffic light experiences, the times when circumstances, people or God, are saying 'STOP' with a big red light. There are 'GO' times too when the green light spurs us into action. The combination of red and amber takes us to anticipation, but how careful we have to be not to rush ahead, jump the lights, or haste may take us to disaster. And there is the amber light that says 'slow down, prepare to wait': a reminder that there are things we cannot fight but must accept.

Each phase has its positive gifts and its frustrations. At one time in my life, my journey to work every day took me to a particular set of traffic lights. My heart would sink if I saw a queue of cars along the motorway exit, because at these lights 'green' was so short that only three or four cars would ever get through at a time, and the next red light would last for absolutely ages. One day, realizing my own impatience, and stuck at the red light, I timed it. It was at red for under two minutes (rather than my imaginary five or six). I had to laugh at myself, and I asked myself exactly why it annoyed me to have to sit still for less than two minutes? From that point on, those lights never bothered me again, I simply stopped and let go into the moment.

What you need

- A large piece of paper
- Coloured pens, including black, green, red and orange
- Or a picture of some traffic lights placed in the middle of a sheet of paper

The exercise

Using your felt pens, or your pictures, mark out four sets of lights on your paper, red, red and amber, green, amber. Think about the sequence of the traffic lights, using some of the questions below. Different areas of your life might be in different places from others, and identifying these might bring a bit more clarity to a complex situation.

Green

- What areas of my life are on GO?
- Where is there energizing movement, or flow?
- Am I under pressure anywhere?
- Am I looking at a green light but not moving forward? Why not?

Red

- What is saying STOP to me right now?
- What is holding me up?
- Where can I not move forward?
- Where am I content to accept stability?
- Where am I stuck?

Amber

- Where do I need to slow down?
- What warning signs do I discern in my life?
- Are there some areas in which I need to ease off?
- Can I renegotiate any aspects of my work?
- Are there commitments that need to change?
- Am I driving myself too hard anywhere?

Red and amber

- Where do I need to get ready to move?
- Am I alert, ready to respond?
- Is my inner world in order?
- What external preparations do I need to make?
- Am I communicating with those around me?

As you prayerfully reflect on these points, write or draw around the four sets of lights, noting circumstances, people, questions that seem important to you.

Reflection

Look at your paper and quietly consider what you notice about it. Where is the energy? If someone else showed you this, what might you say to them? Does anything challenge or surprise you?

You may find that different areas of life are at different sets of traffic lights. With all this in mind, what are your priorities right now? Who is travelling with you? Do you need to talk to them about what the lights mean?

Take your reflection into prayer, adding your own words to complete the following:

- O God, where my life is at GO I need courage to act, strength to keep going, and ...
- Where I see a red light give me grace to STOP, especially ...

- Are you prompting me to notice the amber light, SLOW DOWN, and listen to ...?
- Thank you for the signal that says GET READY. Give me wisdom for ...

In a group

As this is quite a visual exercise people may find it fun to share their reflections with one another. Be sensitive to the possibility of disturbing 'red lights' which people may be living with.

20

Stained glass window

When we know that the light of God is shining upon us, in and through our lives, we feel full of gratitude, joy and a sense of being blessed. We are confident of God's guidance and presence and delighted with all that we are being given. But when we walk through the valley, or the dark night, we wonder where God went and whether there is any purpose or meaning in what seems to be happening. For much of our lives, these two threads may be woven together, in a weaving that in itself raises further questions.

This reflection is about that mix of delight and question, sunshine and shadow, using the metaphor of a stained glass window, through which the light shines sometimes brightly, sometimes dimly. I came across this exercise when it was used on a course I was on many years ago, and it has proved to be a powerful tool for me ever since.

What you need

- A large sheet of paper, preferably A2
- Coloured pens

The exercise

Draw a circle in the centre of the paper, big enough to write a few words or draw a picture in. Around this, arrange a ring of seven circles, and then a second ring of seven circles beyond that. You can then enclose all 15 circles within a large circle to create your window frame.

There are three stages to this reflection, but before you begin, spend some time in stillness. You could ponder a Bible passage such as Psalm 139 or listen to some music, or simply enter into silence. Ask God to guide your reflections and to give you a discerning heart, to know what is important and what is not.

The first stage is the central circle. Draw or write something in the circle that expresses your place of deepest encounter with God, a place of knowing you are in God and loved by God. This may be a physical place you have been to and return to in your imagination and memory, or it may be somewhere you still go to, a 'thin place' where you are particularly conscious of God's presence. The 'place' might not be physical at all; it could be something to do with the sacraments, the cross, or some symbol of your faith. It might be a special Bible verse, hymn, poem or work of art. Whatever it is, it is where you 'go' to reconnect with God and all that holds and sustains you.

When you are ready for the next stage, look at the outer ring of seven circles. These represent the places in your life where the light of God shines through clearly and brightly, where you experience joy and where your faith and hope seem strong. These are areas where you are confident that God is at work in and through your life, leading to gratitude and thanksgiving. In each of these seven circles, write or draw something to express these areas. They may include work, vocation, family, the natural world, leisure activities, your community, your experience, other people, anything at all. Don't think too hard about this; let the Spirit lead you and go with what emerges for you rather than trying to make a list before you begin.

Finally, turn your attention to the inner ring of circles, immediately around your centre. These represent the parts of your window that are darker glass, frosted panes perhaps, in deep shades. They may have a kind of beauty, but the light does not shine through so brightly and at times may seem to be obscured altogether. Ask yourself:

- Where in my life do I struggle to see the light of God?
- Are there areas of deep darkness where I cannot see God's love for me or purpose in my life?
- Where are the puzzles, the griefs, the ongoing intractable circumstances that evoke the question, 'What are you doing God?'
- Where are the areas I find it difficult to believe that God can do anything?

In these seven circles, express something of these areas of your life. Again, do not think too hard about it, and go with whatever honestly comes to mind. Don't censure yourself; if a particular relationship or circumstance comes to mind that is an area of shade, reflect on this without feeling guilty or thinking, 'I can't put that'.

When you have finished your window, take time to gaze at your work and allow the Spirit to deepen your understanding. You may like to ponder these points:

- What was easy about this?
- What was painful or challenging?
- Where was I joyful?
- Where was I reluctant, resistant, angry, sad or afraid?
- Do I connect with my centre enough?
- What do I have to give thanks for?

- Can I trust that God may be somehow present in even the darkest glass?
- As I consider ways forward in my life, what might I need to change or develop?
- How can I take this window into prayer?
- Where is the gift in this picture for me today?

Further reflection

If you look at a large rose window in a cathedral, you have to stand a long way back to get the best view of it. The whole effect is very beautiful, though each small part is beautiful in its way too. We need a sense of perspective in our lives and sometimes it is important to remember the big picture, and to know that all these elements of 'light' are present in our lives. The centre is key and draws our eye back again and again. The dark glass sits between that centre and the outer ring where there is abundant light. Thus the darkness may be diminished, or at least held, and by the grace of God we find hope.

In a group

This is a good exercise to do with a group if you have a long enough session. It would be useful to have prepared handouts with the circles laid out; you will probably need to put this on A4 paper for practical reasons even though that limits the space. Do not explain the whole process in one go; it is best to explain the 'centre' first and ask people to go away and work with this on their own for at least 20 minutes, maybe longer if possible. Then explain the outer circle, allowing plenty of time to consider the areas of sustenance and nourishment in life, and finally attend to the darker and more shaded areas.

It is possible to spend an afternoon or even most of a day on these reflections. You could design a quiet day around this structure, with provision of some liturgy and prayers.

21

Cut-out people

One thing I used to like doing as a child was to cut out little people in a paper chain or circle. Starting with folded paper, you draw a single figure and cut it out. The secret is not to cut round their hands; as long as you make sure the arms are linked, they will still be connected when you unfold the paper.

A sense of call is never an individual thing; the journey is shared by many others. From the very first stirrings of a new sense of vocation, we will be conscious of the impact on those around us and we will need their support. We may be worried about how loved ones will react, yet we may well find that they are not surprised at all and had been wondering when we would get the message ourselves. Others may have to be very gentle when exploring a call, because their loved ones may be horrified at the potential disruption, and may even feel that God is being unreasonable or 'selfish'. Members of families, in particular, may be thrilled, or they may feel threatened and anxious. Friends may be supportive or sceptical; interestingly, it is often those who do not claim to have any particular faith who are most encouraging.

This exercise allows us to recognize and remember those who travel with us and to pray for them. It challenges us to consider where we might need fellow travellers in the future, to seek them out and accept their support.

What you need

- A large square sheet of paper, not too thick, such as flip-chart paper cut off to a square

- A pencil and a pair of scissors
- Coloured pens

The exercise

Take your square of paper and fold it in half diagonally, then fold this in half again. Repeat this a number of times, depending on the size of the paper. You will end up with something that looks like an ice cream cone. On the front of this, draw the outline of a person. The arms must go all the way to the folds at the edge of the section you are drawing on. Now carefully cut round your figure, ensuring that you do not cut across the ends of the 'hands', so the folds hold it all together. You can keep the feet connected as well if you wish and this will make the end result a bit stronger. When you open out your paper you should have a circle of people holding hands. If it does not work the first time, don't worry – you can probably see where you went wrong and have another go. If you fold and cut carefully you might now have a ring of 16 little people.

Now, look at your circle of figures and prayerfully consider who is in your circle. Imagine yourself in the middle. Who might be around you? Write a name on each figure, or use each figure to represent a group, such as 'my children' and write all their names together on one figure. You might include friends, family, soul friends, your pastor, those who are helping you discern the way forward, work colleagues and so on. If you have quite a number of figures in your circle, also include people who have supported and accompanied you in the past. Remember them with thanks, especially if they are no longer with you. Leave one figure blank.

Put your circle down and have a look at it. Who do you want to thank God for? Who would you especially like to pray for? The blank figure is to represent people you have not yet met. Ask God to bring the right people across your path at the right time.

Further reflection

Might you be in someone else's circle? Pray for them now. Ponder these words from Kabir Helminski:

> To approach the Work alone is not only a great limitation, but it runs the risk of cultivating self importance and self righteousness. Spiritual attainment apart from other human beings is illusory and incomplete.[32]

In a group

Have some flip-chart paper or similar already squared off and demonstrate how to fold it, draw a figure and cut it out. There are some popular sculptures of figures holding hands in a circle, and one of these might be a good centre focus. One way to finish would be to give each person a tea light to place in the centre of their circle as part of your closing prayers.

---

32 Helminski, *Living Presence*, p. 14.

22

Circle me, God

Circling prayers are associated with the Celtic tradition in spiritu-ality. Many contemporary prayers, for example in the work of David Adam, repeatedly pray, 'Circle me, Lord'. These prayers often ask for protection, healing, strength or forgiveness. To know that God encircles us can be a source of comfort, especially when we are afraid or anxious, lost or vulnerable. Circles hold, include, contain and secure, yet there is space within them for movement. They have no beginning or end, no straight lines or edges, reminding us of eternity, flow, dance.

In our anxious and sometimes driven lives we might do well to think about the circles rather than the straight lines, which sug-gest beginnings and endings, goals and destinations, time-limited possibilities.

Thinking about life as a straight line means that we will be ever conscious of how far we might be along that line. As we tread the path we will look backwards, sometimes with regret, or perhaps with a sense of peace and happiness. We will also look forward, towards good times with hope and excitement, or with an increasing awareness that we are hurtling towards an end point we cannot avoid.

To see life as a circle gives it a completely different perspective. No amount of creative imagination will change the fact that we are born, live for the time we are given, and then must die. How-ever, to understand our life as a circle enables us to see all our yesterdays and tomorrows as gifts that we hold in the present moment.

This reflection is an invitation to see life in that circular, encompassing perspective, and then to see that there is room still for what needs to make the circle complete, thus discovering and deepening our sense of vocation.

What you need

- A large piece of paper or card, flip-chart size or at least A2
- Coloured pens

The exercise

You need to draw a large circle on your sheet of paper. Leave a small space of an inch or two in the outline between where your pen begins and where it comes almost full circle. You can draw the circle freehand, or use a large plate to draw round. Alternatively, tie a piece of string to your pen, and hold the end of the string in the middle of your paper while you draw the edge of the circle with the pen. You may not produce a mathematically perfect circle, but it will be fine for this exercise.

The gap between where your pen began and where it stopped allows a space that represents the threshold we cross when we draw our last physical breath. Although there is a sense in which we come 'full circle', we also have to recognize that something has happened; we cannot have our time back, even when our lives are looked at from an eternal perspective. Leave this gap for now; you can return to it later and consider what it means for you and how you might express your understanding of this threshold.

Now look at the empty space within the circle. This is all that your life includes in the past, present and future. In the circle, write or draw about your life, with its achievements, relationships, learning, gifts and experience. Ask yourself:

- What are the things I have accomplished?
- What might I be remembered for?

- What aspects of my personality do I value?
- What have I given from my life and experience?
- Who have I been, and who do I still hope to become?
- Are there things I hope to do or be?

When you have finished, your circle may be pretty filled up – with people, places, experiences, hopes and many things that are important to you.

Take a good look at it all and ask this question of yourself, praying for spiritual insight and wisdom: 'What's missing?'

What's missing could be many things. Something unresolved, incomplete, unfinished? This might be a piece of work, an aspect of inner growth, something practical or perhaps spiritual. When you have an idea of what might be missing, consider whether this is something that now needs your attention in some way. Is this an aspect of your sense of vocation? How might you take this forward?

When you are ready to move on, return to the gap between where your circle began and the point where it could be closed. What would you like to put in this space? Do you have a metaphor or image for that threshold? What are your beliefs about what happens in that space?

Further reflection

It may be that you feel nothing at all is 'missing'. If this is true for you then you are blessed indeed (or very self-satisfied!). This exercise is an invitation to consider how we might bring new threads into our lives, or weave in some loose ones. However, if we are able to live in the present, we will know that at any one moment our lives are in fact complete. If we know that we are 'enough' and yet have a sense of direction and purpose for tomorrow then we will be free to live each day fully.

In a group

This reflection could be a deep one, requiring considerable care and sensitivity. There may be those present who are holding issues of illness, death and bereavement. In any group some members will be particularly conscious of the circle of life, its beginnings and endings. If you have a whole day, consider having a portable labyrinth available, or you may be able to hold the day in premises where there is a labyrinth you can use. See the Resources section for information about labyrinths.

23

Wagon wheel

If you are wondering what your call or vocation might be, or considering a change of direction, you will know that there are many things to weigh up. Your deepest sense of motivation, energy, meaning will be what keeps you going in challenging times, so you need to know what that is and how to draw on it. You will draw on everything that you have learnt from life – joys, sorrows, failures and frustrations, achievements, training and education. All this will have equipped you in a variety of ways for what you are called to do and to be.

This reflection invites you to reflect on ways in which your varied life experience, when accepted, integrated and learnt from, becomes foundational for the way in which you live now, informing the expression of your unique gifts and ministry.

What you need

- A large sheet of paper, at least A2
- Coloured pens
- Tea light or candle and matches

The exercise

First, draw the outline of your 'wagon wheel'. It needs a hub, so draw a circle about the size of a saucer, depending on the size of your paper, to represent this. It needs to be big enough to write a few words in or draw a picture. Then draw a circle as large as your paper will allow; either do this freehand, or you can use string tied to your pen to be more accurate. Inside this draw another circle, about an inch smaller, so that you create a 'rim' for your wheel. Leave the space where the spokes would normally go empty for now.

Next, take some time in a quiet and reflective space to prayer-fully consider the following three areas – hub, spokes, rim – allowing plenty of time. Do not rush; it could take a couple of hours or more.

First, look at the hub in the centre of your wheel. Here, write or draw something that summarizes what 'holds you together'. You may think of several things, but aim to focus on what is most fundamental of all. What sustains you in the deepest, most essential and life-giving way?

Try and be specific; the first thought that comes to you might be quite general (such as 'God' or 'nature'). Can you go deeper and identify what it is about what you have named that is most life-giving? A number of the exercises in this book ask a very similar question about your reference point, or centre of meaning, and that is because we all need a spiritual 'home' where we make sense of our world, and find hope, healing and fresh energy.

When you are ready, turn your attention to the 'spokes' of your wheel. These will represent the things, people, circumstances, experiences that you have been shaped by and learnt from. Notice what occurs to you today, without analysing what 'should' be there. You can draw in as few or as many as you wish, but be discerning; you do not have to include everything. A spoke might be something general, such as 'growing up in Wales', or specific, such as 'failing my driving test'. What has been really formative for you? Focus on what memory and imagination naturally brings to your mind. Don't rush this, allowing your heart and intuition to guide you. Draw a spoke for each learning experience you want to include, and write a word or two along it. Use a ruler if you like to be neat, but the point is not to create a beautiful end result so much as to remember and appreciate the riches of your experi-ence. Include great joys, crushing defeat, and even plain boredom

– whatever your inner wisdom offers you. If you find yourself overly discouraged as you ponder your experiences you might like to look at the 'Compost' exercise before returning to this one. Remember, nothing is wasted.

After a while, you will have as many spokes as you wish, or as many as will fit. Now take some time to stop and notice what is there. When you are ready, begin to consider what these experiences have given you. Ask yourself:

- What gifts do I now have, what abilities, skills, capacities or empathies have become part of what I give to others?
- What scars or vulnerabilities do I carry?

Our frailties can be gifts too; they can keep your mind supple and your heart compassionate. Use the rim of your wheel to write some words expressing what gifts you have been given, remembering that some may be gifts of weakness as well as strength.

When you have finished, light a tea light or candle and place it on the hub, giving thanks to God for the gift of integration, recycling and healing.

Further reflection

Anthony de Mello points out that painful events can lead to growth:

> Think of some of the painful events in your life. For how many of them are you grateful today, because thanks to them you changed and grew? Here is the simple truth of life that most people never discover. Happy events make life delightful but they do not lead to self-discovery and growth and freedom. That privilege is reserved to the things and persons in situations that cause us pain.
>
> Every painful event contains in itself a seed of growth and liberation. In the light of this truth return to your life now and take a look at one or another of the events that you are not grateful for, and see if you can discover the potential for growth that they contain which you were unaware of and therefore failed to benefit from. Now think of some recent event that caused you pain that produced negative feelings in you. Whoever or whatever caused those feelings was your teacher, because they revealed so much to you about yourself but you probably did not know. And they offered you an invitation and a challenge to self-understanding, self-discovery, and therefore to growth and life and freedom.[33]

---

33 Anthony de Mello, *The Way to Love*, Image Books, Doubleday, 1995, p. 157.

24

Yes, but ...

'Yes, but ...' is one of those expressions that seem entirely reasonable on our own lips, but strangely infuriating when offered to us from someone else as an excuse or explanation, especially if we really want to say, 'Come on, there is no *but* ... just do it!' When we are faced with the possibility of change, a sense that God might be calling us to something new, we can find that we are conflicted. Our difficulty is not that the sense of call is entirely unthinkable and out of the question. If it was, we might be able to dismiss it completely, at least for a while. In the land of 'yes, but ...' we 'get it', knowing that there is mileage in this new possibility, and we accept that we need to give it serious consideration. Since we cannot come up with an immediately reasonable way of saying no, we play for time instead. Perhaps we hope that by gaining some days, months or years, the idea will go away altogether. God might forget, give up, or ask someone else. However, you do not have to read very far into the Bible to notice that this does not generally happen.

This reflection invites us to own up to our 'yes, but ...' excuses and consider how convincing they might be, to ourselves, to others, and to God. A 'yes, but ...' is not necessarily a bad or a wrong response; it might be an expression of wise caution, or reflect an appropriate consideration for others. But sometimes we need to smile at that 'yes, but ...' and hear God asking: 'Really?'

What you need

- A large sheet of paper, at least A2
- Coloured pens

The exercise

It's important for this exercise to have a big piece of paper. You need lots and lots of space for this, so that you can get every single 'excuse' down, no matter how ridiculous, embarrassing or 'silly'. Usually when we say, 'I am just being silly', what we really mean is that although it seems important to us, we are afraid that others will laugh at us.

So, now is the time to cast aside those inhibitions and give yourself time to own up to all the 'yes, but ...' things that are around for you. When you articulate these excuses, they will often shrivel in the light of day and no longer seem like obstacles or impediments at all.

Take your sheet of paper and some different coloured pens. Consider what it is that you feel God may be calling you to do. Perhaps it is something you have been avoiding really thinking about for a while. Take some moments to close your eyes and hear that prompt or nudge. Someone once described a sense of call as being like a phone ringing in another room – near enough to hear but far enough away to try and ignore, hoping that it will stop or that someone else will pick it up. You might tell yourself that it will ring off before you get there, and in any case it will be for someone else, not you. However, that phone in another room just keeps going. It might stop for a while, but before long it will start up again. There comes a point when you know you will have to answer it, though you are still preparing to say 'wrong number' or 'she's not here'.

Now that you are hearing that insistent, if distant, sense of call, pay attention to it and notice your inner responses. Write down, not as a neat list but all over the page, with different colours and maybe pictures, all the things that come into your mind as 'yes, but ...' responses. Let the colour and size of your writing, as well as where you place the words on the page, reflect how you think and feel. Do not edit or refuse anything that pops up, give it all a place on your sheet.

After a while, when you have run out of things to add, take time to sit and notice what you have written. In the light of everything in front of you, write an appropriate prayer. It might be a prayer of commitment, a prayer asking for help, a prayer for others who are sharing your journey, or perhaps all of those things.

You may like to talk about this further with a spiritual director. Is there anything you need to do next?

Further reflection

Someone once said to me, 'We all come to God with a "but...".' The 'but' may, however, be a gift if we allow it to search us out. Engaging with the 'but' can be like being emptied out, scoured inside, with no inner place left to hide. This is a deeply uncomfortable process, and yet there is a kind of relief and healing in the honesty it requires. When we have voiced the 'but' and been surprised, perhaps, by the grace of God we encounter, we have new energy to live, grow and serve, free of a burden we may have carried for a long time.

In a group

You might consider using a Bible study to start the session off, if appropriate. Or you could ask members of the group to think of people they remember in the Bible who said 'yes, but ...' or 'not yet'.

25

Frozen

The technology we have now, for those who are privileged enough to have access to it, makes life fast and efficient. Our expectations for speed are raised when we are used to sorting all kinds of things out on our phones, tablets and computers. But delay and frustration can strike without warning. Suddenly, usually when you are in a hurry to complete a task, up pops the little spinner that means 'wait', and everything is frozen.

That little wheel is irritating because it makes meaningless promises that have no timescale. Perhaps it is meant to be reassuring, designed to indicate that something is happening, and that if you just wait everything will be all right. The problem with this is that our minds are taken out of the present and into a future which may be just 20 seconds away, or may never arrive at all.

The little spinner is one of those 'are we nearly there yet?' or 'yes, in a minute' or 'your call is important to us' frustrations in daily life. We have no idea whether it really means anything, when it will stop, whether it is going anywhere, or if the system is really broken. What shall I do? Wait a little longer? I might be wasting another 5 minutes of my life. Go back to the previous page, reload, switch off, try again? This could work, but having spent the time it takes to get to this point I might just be further back again in the queue of invisible and unknowable cyber events. Or perhaps it will help to press a few buttons, try moving things around? This is usually not possible, however, because by this time, everything is likely to be frozen and you are stuck.

The worst thing about that little spinner is that it is moving, and this has a mesmerizing effect. The movement convinces us that something is actually happening, but often, the little spinner does not tell the truth; it captivates and deceives us for no good purpose at all.

There are times when life offers up that little spinner in some form or other. We wait for something we believe and hope might, or could, be imminent. However, we don't really know what to expect, and in the meantime our attention is constantly drawn to the email, the phone, the letterbox, or whatever portal might be the delivery point of something that will change our lives. We may become distracted, anxious, depressed, even despairing. We may try and pray, but we cannot settle. We may try and sleep, but we are disturbed. It is not comfortable to have no power to make things shift and get them sorted out, so perhaps we poke at the situation in some way to try and hurry it along. We want answers, results, clarity, peace, but all the time the spinner is saying 'not yet, nearly there, any minute, hold on a bit ...'

Here is a meditation for that little spinner. It can be quite hard to do because it is about stilling what can have power over us. However, that power is illusory and we can let go of the anxiety and frustration it so often evokes.

What you need

- A large sheet of paper
- Coloured pens

The exercise

In the middle of your paper draw a picture of the little spinner. Now use the space around it to record all the things that you are waiting for – everything you want, wish for, are agonizing about and are impatient for. You might write, 'I want John to get a new job' or 'I wish we could book a holiday' or 'I wish I knew if I had passed' or 'I want this house sale to go through'. You could use pictures as well, but it is important to include the desiring words: I long, I hope, I am desperate for, I need, I want, I wish, I can't wait for ... The root of our distress is usually in our immersion in that sense of desire. This can include quite a physical sensation, so note that too: 'I feel sick because ...'

When you have finished, take time to look at what you have written down. Maybe you have one big anxiety in your life at the moment, maybe there are a number.

Now ... for a few moments simply imagine that spinner in the middle going round and round and round, holding all these aspects of your life in stress-creating, sleep-depriving, anxiety-increasing tension. This is what it is like, this is what you are struggling with, and it can be very unpleasant indeed.

Close your eyes (but read the next bit before you actually do!). In your mind see the little spinner doing its thing – and then, in your imagination, freeze it. Yes, stop it; see it come to a complete halt and become inactive. This will happen if you allow it. Then hold the image of a 'not moving at all' spinner in your mind and pay attention to the stillness.

If you can stay with the stillness of that image for just a few moments, you may notice that you are no longer being promised an illusory future. There is only this moment. Your mind has been taken out of the frustration of desiring a future that refuses to arrive and into this space in which, in fact, nothing whatsoever is happening. Now you are simply being open to a different energy, the energy of this moment.

Nothing is happening. This moment contains all you need. The present is complete. The spinner has stopped and you are free of its tyranny.

Of course, it won't take much to start the little thing off again, but as soon as you find your mind being drawn back into future-focused impatience and anxiety, repeat this exercise. Close your eyes, freeze the spinner completely, allow your mind to return to this moment and pay attention. Nothing is happening, and that is all right.

The capacity for living in the present is often called 'mindfulness'.

> Mindful awareness – or mindfulness – spontaneously arises … when we learn to pay attention, on purpose, in the present moment, without judgement, to things as they actually are … In mindfulness, we start to see the world as it is, not as we expect it to be, how we want it to be, or what we fear it may become.[34]

Prayer

God, I allow your stillness to seep into me. I receive it as gift. I cannot know anything beyond this moment and your presence in it. Let that be enough for me.

In a group

You could read the first part of the exercise to the group, or you could give a short talk in your own words using the idea of the spinner to illustrate the difficulties of anxiety and impatience. Then give the group large sheets of paper and pens and allow them time to get their experiences down. After a little while, perhaps 15–30 minutes, depending on the kind of group and how long you have, draw them back together. Take them through

---

34 Mark Williams and Danny Penman, *Mindfulness*, Piatkus, 2011, p. 35.

the meditation of seeing the spinner and allowing it to 'freeze' quite slowly. As a leader, you will also need to visualize this very strongly for yourself, because if you are immersed in this exercise, you will be able to lead the group into an authentic experience.

Allow a time of silence. The length of this will depend on whether the group is used to this kind of meditation, and other factors too, so you must discern what is appropriate.

After a period of time very gently re-engage the group, perhaps by fading in a suitable piece of music and/or praying the prayer above, or another suitable prayer. You might choose to read a piece of Scripture or invite the group to quietly sing together.

Be aware that while this may be helpful for some, it takes a bit of practice to slow down and enter the present in this way. The meditation cannot solve problems that are very real, but it may enable someone to step back a little from the anxiety and panic and engage with the present moment.

26

What time is your life?

Time is a funny thing. It seems to go at different speeds depending on the circumstances: how old we are, whether we are waiting for something, dreading something, or just bored. We all know how true it is that time is precious and the minutes we have don't come round again. Yet we also know that time can seem tyrannical with its incessant marking of minutes and seconds that can make us anxious. Suppose there was no time, only the reality of the present moment? We would be just as we are, we would still age, but we might worry less about where we are on the ever-moving line from birth to death, and simply accept that now is now.

This is one version of a well-known exercise that invites us simply to think about the present moment and what it might mean for us. We cannot ignore the past or the future but we can get them in perspective. We should not be intimidated by concepts of 'too soon' or 'too late' or 'it's not a good time right now'. What will we do with the precious time that is given to us?

What you need

- A sheet of paper, A5 or A4 is sufficient
- Coloured pens

The exercise

For this exercise you need to draw a simple outline of a clock face on your paper, with numbers round the outside but no hands. Don't make it too small.

Take some time to look at your clock face. It has no hands, so it could be any time in the day or the night. Consider the question, 'What time is it in your life?' The question has nothing at all to do with how old you are. Rather, the question is about the experience and opportunities which you hold in your hands. It is not about age, but about perspective.

A young woman asked her great-grandmother to come to the birthday party she was planning many months in advance. Great-grandmother looked sad and disappointed, saying that she did not think she would make it. Mindful of the lady's great age and increasing frailty, the young woman chided her great-grandmother and said, 'Oh don't say that, you will be with us a long time yet.' Realizing the misunderstanding, the old lady burst into a fit of laughter and said, 'Oh no, dear, I am going on a cruise next year.' She had plenty of living still to do.

Different life stages can mean different and quite unexpected, even illogical things to different people. For example, one person may look at retirement and it will seem like 10 a.m., while for another it will feel like 5 p.m. or perhaps 9 p.m. or even 2 a.m., all for very different reasons.

A young person will not necessarily choose a 'morning' time, nor an older person a 'late' time. We have complex feelings about our lives, and are affected by the interaction of circumstances, health, work, relationships, leisure, families, bereavement, and much more.

The way to approach this is not to think about it or reason it out. Take some time now to be still and listen to your own inner wisdom. Ask yourself, 'What time is it in my life?' and allow an idea to be given to you, not by working it out, but from the deep place where the Spirit guides you. This is an intuitive exercise, which invites you to get in touch with something you already know but may not have named, or given any thought to.

Without analysing, judging, calculating, or stopping to consider whether you like your answer, allow your time of day to present itself to your imagination and draw some hands on your clock.

When you have drawn them in, sit with your image for a while and prayerfully consider the following questions:

- What does 'my' time of day feel like?
- What does this time mean to me?
- How does this time of day challenge me?

Further reflection

Time becomes the byword for all that troubles us and causes us stress and annoyance. It takes us captive and makes us into its slaves. Hence we long to take time off, to have time for myself and to be not working against the clock. Indeed, the whole notion of the holiday has become for us the fixed time that we are 'let off' the normal strict demands of time. Conversely, if we have time on our hands, we are bad or useless or both. So time – measured sequences outside of us, tells us what we should be doing, when we should do it, and becomes our accuser if we are not in its power.[35]

Ponder these words from Thomas Merton:

We cannot master everything, taste everything, understand everything, drain every experience to the last dregs. But if we have the courage to let almost everything else go, we will probably be able to retain the one thing necessary for us – whatever it may be. If we are too eager to have everything, we will almost certainly miss even the one thing we need.

Happiness consists in finding out precisely what the 'one thing necessary' may be in our lives and in gladly relinquishing all the

---

35 Thomas O'Loughlin, *Journeys on the Edges*, DLT, 2000, p. 133.

rest. For then, by a divine paradox, we find the everything else is given to us together with the one thing we needed.[36]

In a group

You could have some handouts with a clock face (without hands) ready. Introduce the exercise and be sure that everyone under- stands that age is not necessarily at all relevant. Be gently aware that there could be people in the room who have been bereaved, or who have life-limiting conditions, or have loved ones who do. This can be a powerful exercise if people are engaging with big questions about life and death, health, retirement or transition and it is important to introduce the exercise in an atmosphere of prayerful and spacious stillness. It is simple to explain, but do not rush and don't assume that everyone will find it easy. If the ques- tion is put too abruptly some may find it disturbing, so speak in a gentle and measured way and engage the group gradually in the task so that they have to think, 'Ah yes, I see where this is going, I can do that.'

Depending on the group and the context, you could allow them to complete their papers quickly where they are, or encourage them to find a personal space for 10 minutes or more before returning. When the group gathers again you may wish to ask for general comments or reflections by simply asking, 'How did you get on?' Make it clear that you are not asking people to share what they have as their time, and that not everyone has to speak. You could leave out any discussion at all and draw the group back together in silence. You could light a candle in the centre of the group and invite them to fold up their paper, write their name on the outside and place it around the candle as a sign of commit- ment to God's way for them, whatever time it is. You could play some music and end with a simple prayer.

---

36 Thomas Merton, *No Man is an Island*, Burns and Oates, 1955, p. 114.

Prayer

O God, you are inside and outside time, and altogether timeless. Release us from our preoccupations and anxieties, our boredom, impatience and regret. In your Spirit give us hope and joy to celebrate each moment, refusing limitation and fear, ever open to the unimagined and timeless. Amen.

27

Windows

What do you see when you look out of the window? I am fortunate enough to live in a house where I can see fields from every window. This might not be everyone's idea of a view but I delight in the sight of red kites overhead, nuthatches and long-tailed tits on the bird feeder, and sheep, cows and horses over the road. What we see from our windows are sometimes those things just beyond our boundaries. We may have a connection with them but they don't quite belong to us. Or they may be things that intrude, disturb and distract because we have no control over them. We may see things from our windows that we cannot reach or aspire to, whether it is the fancy car heading down the road, or the far mountains we don't have the strength to climb. We might also notice the permanence and reassurance of what we can see – the trees that are older than we are and will probably be here after us, the moon on a clear but sleepless night, the sun, and the way the light and shade in our lives changes with the seasons.

This exercise is a reflection on the things we see from the windows of our lives, and it offers an opportunity to simply stop and reflect. We might then have cause to give thanks, to pray for someone, perhaps to discern whether we need to take some kind of action.

Windows in our buildings are very important and it is interesting to note how they vary in style and size. Big office blocks seem to be all window. A tiny cottage with thick walls in an exposed location might have very small windows. Changing your windows can change your house completely. If you have not cleaned them for a while and then you finally get around to it – wow! What a difference. Suddenly there is light and clarity you did not realize you were missing.

Awareness means to watch, to observe what is going on within you and around you. 'Going on' is pretty accurate: Trees, grass, flowers, animals, rock, *all* of reality is moving. One observes it, one watches it. How essential it is for human beings not just to observe himself or herself, but to watch all of reality. Are you imprisoned by your concepts? Do you want to break out of your prison? Then *look*; observe; spend hours observing. Watching what? *Anything*. The faces of people, the shapes of trees, a bird in flight, a pile of stones, watch the grass grow. Get in touch with things, look at them ... what will we see? This thing that we choose to call reality, whatever it is beyond words and concepts. This is a spiritual exercise – connected with spirituality – connected with breaking out of your cage, out of the imprisonment of the concepts and words.[37]

What you need

- A place to sit by a window – it does not matter what the view is
- Your journal or a notebook
- Pen or pencil
- A candle and matches (optional)

The exercise

Find a window where you can be relaxed, comfortable and where you won't be disturbed for a while. It does not have to be a beautiful view; it could be a very ordinary outlook.

What kind of window is this? Notice whether it is old or new, large or small, clean or dirty. You might like to light a candle in front of this window. It has become an icon and now you can look into and through it.

---

37 Anthony de Mello, *Awareness*, HarperCollins, 1997, p. 127.

Look out of the window. Take time now to notice, with a soft but attentive gaze, everything. Don't think about it, just notice, and notice some more. As you simply look, your mind will slow down and become receptive to detail and nuance, to light and shade and small things.

You may wonder why you are doing this, and what the point is, but stay with the moment and be attentive to all that you can see and hear. Notice where the boundaries of your view are, let what is out of sight go and stay present to what you can see.

After a while, when you are centred and still and feel 'at home' in this noticing place, ask the view, 'What is your gift to me?' This may seem like a very odd thing to say but in this moment you are very present, in God, to the God-given context in which you are placed. You, and all that you can see, belong to God and there is a gift for you here, though you may have no idea what it is. Allow your attention to be drawn to the gift; you may find that whatever that gift is, it is exactly what you need for today.

What is this gift for? Is it something that changes your outlook and perspective, takes you into prayer, or challenges your life in some way?

Write in your journal or notebook anything that seems important.

Further reflection

This exercise is very, very simple but potentially life-changing. I once sat and looked at the view beneath my feet and was given a gift, through what I saw, that changed my whole perspective on a seemingly intractable problem. It did not solve it, but I found a way to live with it. On another occasion, some fresh deep green tulip leaves, bursting out of the soil in a pot on the periphery of my vision, which I had not noticed for 10 minutes even though I was 'looking' out of the window, suddenly entered my awareness and offered an overwhelming gift in the face of great sorrow. Such moments can unlock something within us, opening us to new depths of prayer as we connect more fully with what is going on in and around us. As in dreams, our gaze is drawn to something by intuition, in Spirit-given wisdom and, attending to the insight we are offered, we are led to a deep well of refreshment, encouragement and hope.

28

Whale watching

The story of Jonah is a great one to ponder when you are thinking about the direction of your life and what your vocation might be. The difficulty for many people is that they are not sure what God is saying. Jonah, on the other hand, knew exactly what God was saying, but he did not like it much, and to make the point he took off in the opposite direction as fast as possible. He ended up, helpless, in the dark, after being swallowed by a whale, so the tale goes. He was delivered after three days, a changed man, or partly changed at least. The story of Jonah is a great gift to those who want to run from that uncomfortable sense of God's call; and in trying to renegotiate, they may find that a new sense of call is being brought to birth.

This reflection is about the things we are running from, and what happens in the belly of the whale while we are trying to do so. In that womb-like place of darkness and attempted escape, we are invited to come to terms with our deepest desire, motivation and purpose. Jonah had to confront his fear, resentment and personal responsibility. He had to be willing to give up his agenda, however justified, for one he initially resisted.

The belly of the whale is a place of deep transformation, where we come to an end of ourselves. There is nowhere left to hide, and nothing we can do. In the darkness, there are no reference points and no sense of time. What is happening in this place?

What you need

- A large sheet of paper, A3 or A2
- Coloured pens

The exercise

Lay out the paper 'land-scape' (so that the long edge is towards you). Draw a rough outline of a whale, with plenty of space in the 'belly', leaving some space around the edges of the paper. The picture here is a good shape: the body is the important part. Take some time to be still. You might like to read the story of Jonah. Enter into silence and stillness, and begin to ask these questions:

- Is there resistance in me to some sense of a call from God?
- What am I afraid of?
- What is it that I do not want to do?
- Is there somewhere I do not want to go?

Write these things, with symbols and pictures if you wish, in the space around your 'whale'. Then begin to consider:

- How am I being changed?
- What is being 'birthed' in my life?
- What whispers from God do I hear in the darkness?

Write these things in the 'belly' of the whale. These are the gifts and challenges of time spent in the dark, when nothing seems to be happening and it seems that life may be over.

Spend some time offering up to God the feelings you carry in this space where some new sense of call, some new potential is being prepared for birth. Ask God for whatever it is you need in order to wait in the dark, and then perhaps to embark on a new adventure. This might be an internal adventure of change and growth, or it might be something new you are called to do with your life.

Further reflection

Barbara Brown Taylor offers the thought that the dark is not always unfriendly or unproductive. She writes about a member of the French Resistance, Jacques Lusseyran, who became blind at the age of seven, and his remarkable discoveries about what can be discerned in the dark. Jacques developed an amazing capacity for engaging with the world around him, knowing through sound about the kinds of trees he was among, and the shape and size of walls and furniture. He learnt, too, that he had an inner light, which perceptibly grew or diminished, depending on his own capacity for positive attention.

> In January 1944, the Nazis captured Lusseyran and shipped him to Buchenwald along with two thousand of his countrymen. Yet even there he learned how hate worked against him, not only darkening his world but making it smaller as well. When he let himself become consumed with anger, he started running into things, slamming into walls, and tripping over furniture. When he called himself back to attention, the space both inside and outside of him opened up so that he found his way and moved with ease again. The most valuable thing he learned was that no one could turn out the light inside him without his consent. Even when he lost track of it for a while he knew where he could find it again.[38]

---

38 Barbara Brown Taylor, *Learning to Walk in the Dark*, Canterbury Press, 2014, p. 107.

In the dark, womb-like space of the whale, there is a kind of light. We need to be attentive and still to perceive it. When in the dark, close your eyes, stop straining for signs of light; allow the light within to open up a spacious place in which you can see the way.

Have you ever walked a labyrinth? There are many ways of engaging with a labyrinth (there is more information about labyrinths in the Resources section of this book). If you take a labyrinth walk when you are in a time of 'darkness', here is one way to approach it. As you walk the path of your chosen labyrinth, allow the 'centre' to be the place of darkness for you. As you walk towards it, acknowledge what seems 'dark' to you and allow yourself to notice it, name it and feel it. Don't run away from it or pretend it does not exist, and when you reach the centre, spend some time pondering what this 'belly of the whale' means for you. It can be hard to pray in such a place, and yet sometimes, as Jessica Martin describes:

> At the centre of it there is an experience of meeting God which – in a sense – solves nothing at all, but which is nevertheless soaked in the unsettling clarity of divine presence.[39]

In a group

It is important not to suggest that people end up in a dark place because of 'disobedience' or running away from God. This is not likely to be very helpful. Rather, the belly of the whale can be a place to re-evaluate a sense of call, become still and attentive and perhaps encounter God in a way that allows us to emerge to new possibilities. Be aware that not everyone will want to 'share' this sort of material, and they may not even have words for it, so do not create too much expectation of sharing together unless you are confident it is appropriate.

---

39 Jessica Martin, in Samuel Wells and Sarah Coakley (eds), *Praying for England*, Continuum, 2008, p. 108.

29

Mission statement

What matters ... is the specific meaning of a person's life at a given moment.[40]

The idea of a 'mission statement' has really taken hold, not only for churches and groups for whom 'mission' has a spiritual meaning, but also for charities, businesses, and in fact any group that feels a need to say 'this is who we are, this is what we do, this is where we are going and this is what we want to achieve'. A mission statement may explicitly, or implicitly, say something about values, meaning, direction and purpose. Individuals can have a mission statement too, perhaps as a way of defining and directing a sense of vocation, or even simply as motivation to reach a personal goal.

Victor Frankl believed that 'Man's search for meaning is the primary motivation of his life' and that 'this meaning is unique and specific in that it must and can be fulfilled by him alone. Such is the power of a true sense of meaning that a person will live and die for it.'[41]

In Margaret Craven's short story, *I Heard the Owl Call my Name*, the bishop of a remote, inaccessible community, where the ministry is hard and apparently thankless, reflects that 'for me it has always been easier here, where only the fundamentals count,

---

40 Victor Frankl, *Man's Search for Meaning*, Rider, 2008, p. 113.
41 Frankl, *Man's Search for Meaning*, p. 105.

to learn what every man must learn in this world ... enough of the meaning of life to be ready to die'.[42]

Writing a 'mission statement' challenges you to consider what is most fundamental about the trajectory of your life, what is left when power, choice, even health, is stripped away. What will always hold your focus and your desire? What will keep you energized, praying and motivated, even when your energies and opportunities seem to be diminishing?

Stephen Covey, author of a number of best-selling books on motivation and purpose, writes:

> In order to write a personal mission statement, we must begin at the very centre of our Circle of Influence, that centre comprised of our most basic paradigms, the lens through which we see the world ... Whatever is at the centre of our life will be the source of our security, guidance, wisdom, and power.[43]

Covey suggests that 'security' means our sense of anchorage, our values; 'guidance' represents the source of our sense of direction in life; 'wisdom' is the way we integrate judgement and discernment in a balanced perspective; and 'power' is our energy to act, overcoming old habits and developing more effective ones. In a faith perspective, all these elements will have spiritual depth and meaning, lived out in the light of the 'higher power' which, as 12-step programmes have long recognized, calls us to live in the light of that which is beyond our own resources and capacities.

As Richard Rohr says:

> If we are to come to believe that a Power greater than ourselves can restore us to sanity, then we will come to that belief by developing the capacity for a *simple, clear, and uncluttered presence*. Those who can be present with head, heart, and body at

---

42 Margaret Craven, *I Heard the Owl Call my Name*, Picador, 1980, p. 119.

43 Stephen R. Covey, *Seven Habits of Highly Effective People*, Simon and Schuster, 2004, p. 109.

the same time will always encounter The Presence, whether they call it God or not.[44]

This reflection is about finding and articulating a 'shape' for your sense of direction. A mission statement is a kind of signpost, pointing to the path of what is most important, what is most fundamental about what we are on the earth for.

What you need

- A large sheet of paper, preferably A2
- Coloured pens

The exercise

Take some time to become still and centred. Then jot down on your sheet of paper as many ideas as you can think of in response to the question, 'What am I on the earth for?' This is a question about you in particular, and your life as it is now.

Include all the words that come to mind that have meaning for you, that inspire you. Let these begin to come together in short phrases that sum up what you feel life is all about.

Reflection

A similar idea is the Rule of Life; many religious communities draw up their own Rule in order to give their shared life an agreed shape. 'Rule' might sound rather legalistic to those who have not heard of a Rule of Life before, but the word needs to be understood more as 'measure' or 'map' than 'law'. We sometimes think of 'rules' as things we must be sure to keep, but a Rule of Life is more about signposts than commandments. It is meant to open the way, enabling you to see ways forward, not to restrict

44 Richard Rohr, *Breathing Under Water*, St Anthony Messenger Press, 2011, p. 14.

or constrain you. The short 'Rule for a New Brother', originally written for a Dutch community, expresses this sense beautifully in its gentle call to what matters, not to contain life, but to release it:

You will surely have realised
that you cannot become a spiritual person
without an interior discipline
in your dealings with the world.
Don't let yourself be trapped into the unrest
that comes from the excessive talking and gossiping.

Be discerning in your choice
of what the television, radio and papers offer you.
Without a personal control
on your imagination and emotions
you will undermine your spiritual strength
and lessen your chances
of genuinely meeting and loving one another.[45]

These beautiful words invite rather than prescribe, enlighten rather than control.

A Rule of Life will expand and elaborate on 'how' you might live in the light of your mission statement. A mission statement is like the signpost that says 'The North', whereas a Rule of Life is perhaps like the voice of the satnav suggesting that we 'take the next exit' or maybe 'turn around when possible'!

In a group

Begin with some brief input, drawing on the ideas here. Then allow people some individual time to reflect on the words and phrases that emerge for them. You could then structure a time for people to work in pairs, offering their thoughts to each other and listening without judgement.

45 The Benedictine Nuns of Cockfosters (trans.), *Rule for a New Brother*, DLT, 1973, p. 50.

30

Mandala

The word 'mandala' is Sanskrit for 'circle', and mandalas have long been used in many spiritual traditions. They symbolize the wholeness, unity and integrity of the universe and therefore can be used in art, prayer and meditation in any number of ways. 'Mindfulness' is a concept that has become enormously popular in secular as well as sacred contexts and there are now colouring books available designed for grown-ups that offer mandalas to complete with crayons or pens. Meditating with an existing mandala is one way of praying, and so is the creation of a mandala. Creating your own mandala is an opportunity to spend time making a beautiful design with shapes and colours that appeal to you, or have meaning for you.

This exercise invites you to create your own mandala. Part of the purpose is the reflective and still, intentional space you enter into when you undertake something creative. There are books that explain about geometry, pattern, colour, history and meaning of mandalas, but you do not need to be an expert in these details in order to create a mandala of your own as a way of prayer. Jung was interested in mandalas; they are used in spirituality workshops and in art therapy. Some labyrinths can be understood as a kind of mandala because walking them involves a reflection on the whole of life, where there is connection, memory, energy and hope. Walking a labyrinth is a physical activity which may take you on a similar journey to the one you undertake while making and colouring a mandala. You might notice that several of the exercises in this book make use of circles; the circle is an obvious symbol for wholeness, completeness and integrity, things that we value and hope for, for ourselves and for our world.

Some mandalas and labyrinths are created to be only temporary. Buddhist monks have a tradition of creating beautifully intricate mandalas with coloured sand. Look on the internet and find some amazing examples. They are made with enormous attention to detail and their construction and deconstruction is undertaken with particular ritual. You might have seen labyrinths on a beach, or created from grass cuttings or night lights. Their fragility is part of their meaning.

Many cathedrals have a rose window, which are also a form of mandala, possibly incorporating biblical themes and colours chosen for their spiritual significance.

What you need

- Some white card, at least A4 size
- Pencil and scissors
- Coloured pens

The exercise

Find somewhere quiet where you have a table to work on. Take some time to relax and 'arrive' in this space. You might like to play some music. The first thing you need to do is create the circle that will be your mandala. You could use a pair of compasses, or draw round a large plate. Make your circle as big as you can, then cut it out.

Now you are ready to begin. Before you make any marks, look at your blank circle. Take some time to breathe deeply and put aside the immediate concerns of the day and the rest of life. Expect your imagination and intuition to guide you. When you are ready, take a pencil and make a start on your pattern. You can create your mandala however you like, but traditionally they are symmetrical in design.

The colours, shapes and lines you work with will reflect your inner world. This process can happen quite naturally and the end result may surprise you. At this point the best thing to do is let your imagination run free, just doodle, draw and colour what seems to emerge from within you.

Keep drawing and colouring, being inspired by your inner world of memory, experience, hope, sorrow, and create the shapes, lines and colours that give expression to your thoughts and feelings.

Reflection

When you have finished, tidy up your materials and sit for a while with what you have made. What do you notice about it now you look at the whole thing? Notice where there is energy in your work, whether positive or negative. This might be expressed in the depth of colour, the intensity of lines and shapes, the detail or lack of it, or the speed with which you worked. Does anything surprise you? How might you turn this into a prayer? Do you need to ask for forgiveness, strength, peace? Does your design make you think of anyone you need to pray for? What would you like to give thanks for?

You may like to keep your mandala for a while in your note-book or Bible. It may challenge or comfort you and help you to pray. But do not become too attached to it; be ready to give it up and make a new one when the time is right, one that may be quite different.

In a group

You can introduce the exercise in the way described here, and allow people plenty of time to play with shape and colour. This is not an exercise that can be done quickly. It would work well as an evening activity, ending with Night Prayer.

Bibliography

Neil Astley and Pamela Robertson-Pearce (eds), *Soul Food*, Bloodaxe, 2007
Wilkie Au and Noreen Cannon Au, *The Discerning Heart*, Paulist Press, 2006
Ian Bradley, *Colonies of Heaven*, DLT, 2000
Stephen R. Covey, *Seven Habits of Highly Effective People*, Simon and Schuster, 2004
Margaret Craven, *I Heard the Owl Call my Name*, Picador, 1980
Anthony de Mello, *Awareness*, Harper Collins, 1997
Anthony de Mello, *The Way to Love*, Image Books, Doubleday, 1995
Brian Draper, *Spiritual Intelligence*, Lion, 2009
Brian Draper, *Labyrinth*, Lion, 2010
Victor Frankl, *Man's Search for Meaning*, Rider, 2008
Kahlil Gibran, *The Prophet*, Oneworld Publications, 1998
Kabir Helminski, *Living Presence*, Jeremy P. Tarcher, 1992
Gerard W. Hughes, *God, Where are You?* DLT, 1997
Dennis Linn, Sheila Fabricant Linn, Matthew Linn, *Healing the Purpose of your Life*, Paulist Press, 1999
Gordon MacDonald, *Rebuilding Your Broken World*, Highland Books, revised 2004
Helen Macdonald, *H is for Hawk*, Jonathan Cape, 2014
Dorothy McRae-McMahon, *Prayers for Life's Particular Moments*, SPCK, 2001
Thomas Merton, *New Seeds of Contemplation*, Burns and Oates, 1999 (first published 1962)
Thomas Merton, *No Man is an Island*, Burns and Oates, 1955
Thomas Moore, *Dark Nights of the Soul*, Hachette Digital, 2004
John Moses, *The Desert*, Canterbury Press, 1997
Thich Nhat Hanh, *Essential Writings*, Orbis Books, 2001
Henri Nouwen, *Spiritual Formation*, SPCK, 2011
Thomas O'Loughlin, *Journeys on the Edges*, DLT, 2000
Richard Rohr, *Everything Belongs*, Crossroad Publishing, 1999
Richard Rohr, *Breathing Under Water*, St Anthony Messenger Press, 2011

Richard Rohr and Andreas Ebert, *The Enneagram: A Christian Perspective*, Crossroad, 2001

Ronald Rolheiser, *The Shattered Lantern*, Crossroad Publishing, 2004

Verena Schiller, *A Simplified Life*, Canterbury Press, 2010

Cyprian Smith, *The Way of Paradox*, DLT, 2004

Barbara Brown Taylor, *Learning to Walk in the Dark*, Canterbury Press, 2014

Eckhart Tolle, *A New Earth*, Penguin, 2005

Hannah Ward and Jennifer Wild (eds), *Human Rites*, Mowbray, 1995

Sally Welch, *Walking the Labyrinth*, Canterbury Press, 2010

Samuel Wells and Sarah Coakley (eds), *Praying for England*, Continuum, 2008

Mark Williams and Danny Penman, *Mindfulness*, Piatkus, 2011

The Benedictine Nuns of Cockfosters (trans), *Rule for a New Brother*, DLT, 1973

Jeremy Young, *The Cost of Certainty*, DLT, 2004

Resources

Prayer and meditation

Centering prayer, as taught by Thomas Keating and Basil Pennington: www.contemplativeoutreach.org

World Community for Christian Meditation: Meditation practice, as taught by John Main: www.wccm.org

Spiritual direction

The London Centre for Spirituality has a list of spiritual directors on its website: www.spiritualitycentre.org

If you know which Anglican diocese you live in or near, look at the diocesan website to see if there is a spirituality adviser who can advise you on finding a spiritual director. You do not need to belong to the Church of England to ask for contacts. Your nearest Roman Catholic diocese may have someone you could ask. Also there are local networks in the Methodist, United Reformed and Baptist Churches which you may be able to find with a little internet searching.

Retreats

The Retreat Association: www.retreats.org.uk

The Retreat Association has details of many retreat houses, large and small; some offer programmes and some simply offer space.

You can look for accommodation in a religious community where you can join in the worship, and where meals may be provided, or you may prefer a self-catering space where you can create your own rhythm.

The Enneagram

The Retreat Association has information about where to find an Enneagram-themed retreat.

There are many books offering an introduction. *The Enneagram: A Christian Perspective* by Richard Rohr and Andreas Ebert is particularly useful.

Mandalas

www.creatingmandalas.com
An internet search will bring up various websites, many of which draw on influences outside the Christian tradition and won't therefore appeal to everyone. Do your own search and follow what interests you.

Look in supermarkets and bookshops for Mindfulness colouring books, many of which make use of mandalas.

Have a look at the artwork of Mary Fleeson at the Lindisfarne Scriptorium; elements of the mandala shape can be seen in some of her detailed designs: www.Lindisfarne-scriptorium.co.uk

Labyrinth

Labyrinths have a long history within and beyond the Christian tradition. An internet search will reveal many resources from a variety of perspectives. Two particularly helpful books written from a Christian viewpoint are *Labyrinth: Illuminating the Inner Path* by Brian Draper and *Walking the Labyrinth* by Sally Welch.

Printed in March 2024
by Rotomail Italia S.p.A., Vignate (MI) - Italy